CALL
ENTER

CALL CENTER

A Focus on Customer Service

Gwen Foster Oglesby

BROWN BOOKS
PUBLISHING GROUP

Call Center
A Focus on Customer Service

Brown Books Publishing Group
16250 Knoll Trail Drive, Suite 205
Dallas, Texas 75248
www.BrownBooks.com
(972) 381-0009

A New Era in Publishing®
ISBN 978-1-61254-874-6
Library of Congress Control Number 2016937892

Printed in the United States
10 9 8 7 6 5 4 3 2 1

For more information or to contact the author, please go to www.CallCenterTheBook.com.

I dedicate this book to my daddy, Booker T. Foster Jr. He was by far one of the nicest people who ever graced my life! My mother, Ruth Foster, who is my biggest cheerleader and forever encouraging me in my dreams. My wonderful brothers, Gregory and Gerald Foster, as well as my loving daughter, Corliss Oglesby, who supported me through this entire project. I love you all!

Contents

Acknowledgments

During my call center career, I have worked and collaborated with many talented supervisors and managers who have the awesome responsibility of leading and inspiring their teams. This community of leaders is more than what its title states. We function in multifaceted capacities: counselor, confidant, role model, motivator, heavy-handed enforcer, and, at times, mercy giver. The role of leadership is rewarding, yet challenging and frustrating at times—a roller coaster of emotions. We serve as that "bridge" between the employee and senior management by ensuring our teams understand and support the company's vision and goals. At times, we are held accountable when our team's performance is subpar. We take the hit, but we keep going. On a personal level, these leaders have extended their open arms to me by sharing valuable skills, information, or just a confidential ear to allow me to share my innermost thoughts and frustrations. I salute this community of leaders for the awesome contributions they have made to the customer service industry. We don't get it right all of the time, but I can honestly confirm that the majority of the call center leaders I have worked with are sincere in their role.

The customer service representative is the backbone of the customer service industry. They are tasked to learn particular products, systems, and databases as well as demonstrate call control and empathy in order to resolve the customer's need in a timely manner. It is a demanding job that can go unappreciated. They willingly show support to their coworkers and are readily available to help build a positive workplace culture through various engagement activities. I have worked with so many customer service representatives who willingly provided me with technical support and assistance. For this, I am forever grateful.

Balancing personal responsibilities with work life can be a challenge. My parents provided phenomenal support while my daughter was in grade school. Fortunately, my daughter, Corliss, attended the same elementary school where my mother taught (John E. Ford); all I had to do was get her to school. After school, she would go to my parents' house and get a full meal, and they would take her to any after-school activities. If I had a long workday, she would even spend the night with my parents. When my daughter was in middle school and high school, my father would be at the school on time to get her. What an arrangement and a true blessing! Thank you, Mom and Dad!

I would like to thank the following supervisors and managers who provided their input on chapter 8, Supervisor Amnesty Day: Janice Bing, Reginald Caldwell, Wanda Cassels, Petrona Fletcher, Tina Foster, Chad Fowler, Deionn Glover, Tamra James, Clint Law, David Moses, Herbert Nixon, Monet Pearson, George Reed, Altamese Satterwhite, Verna Summey, Aliza Sylvia, and Regina Thornton. Your input and candor will always be greatly appreciated!

Thank you to Brown Books for giving me a vehicle to voice my passion and for taking a chance on a first-time writer.

Introduction

Every job I have held in my career has been in the customer service industry, with the majority of my professional years spent working in call centers. It is working at call centers where I recall the most memorable employee/customer experiences that shaped my passion for customer service. I should share that being in the role of a customer and encountering poor service and unprofessionalism also heightened this passion. I wholeheartedly believe customers should be treated with the utmost respect and appreciation. Why? They have invested their money for a product or service and have the right to expect proper treatment in return. Customers are also critical to the success of any business, so they should be valued. I have been in a fast food drive-through line where the employee took my money, gave me my food, and just closed the window. No "thank you" or "please come again." I have been in a retail store where the employee did not acknowledge me during the entire checkout process. I have called a company to conduct business over the phone only to find a representative who was neither engaged in the conversation nor helpful. There have been instances when the representative transferred me without advising where or why I was being transferred. I've had a doctor's appointment and sat in the waiting room for long periods of time without anyone from the front desk apologizing for the delay. Let's be frank: we have all experienced poor customer service, whether in a restaurant, retail store, or doctor's office. In these settings where there is face-to-face customer service, you can see the person you are interacting with along with his or her body language and sense of urgency. But when seeking customer service over the phone, you have the added non-visual element that causes you to wonder, *Who is the person on the other side of the phone?* Is he or she trustworthy and accurately handling my request? Does this person even care about my situation and have my best interest at heart? Poor customer service is a growing epidemic. As society's population grows and countries become more modernized, the need for improved customer service will become a mainstay.

The saying is true: if you have worked at one call center, you have worked at them all. I worked at three different call centers in my career and began to notice similarities when sharing performance concerns with fellow supervisors at my first call center job. I began to compile and save my coaching verbiage because these concerns also applied to other team members. When I moved to my second call center role, I again found remarkable similarities across employee behaviors. This confirmed my belief that call centers have a sense of déjà vu. There are usually no surprises but more of a "been there, done that" sentiment. The types of employee performance issues are similar in call centers, which means something is lacking in the call center/customer service arena. Something must be done to improve customer service and reduce the employee drama in the workplace. Something must be done to lower the high turnover rate in call centers. Employees can't continue to leave one call center and work at another only to continue the same negative behaviors. Likewise, employees can't continue to leave one call center for another and experience the same obstacles that prevent them from providing excellent service to their customers.

The intent of this book is to create dialogue and spark self-awareness within all parties on how their individual actions impact others. It's a straight, real-talk book that gives insight on call center dynamics and the practical steps a call center employee must take to succeed on the job. This book will also delve into the obligations of our employers as well as the sometimes unreasonable expectations from our customers—all of which affect the state of customer service. I envision this as an "edutainment" book where employees can receive practical guidance on maintaining a successful career in the workplace in addition to getting a glimpse of the shenanigans some employees will attempt to avoid handling their core responsibilities. It's a learn and laugh, easy-read book. This book includes some actual workplace moments I have encountered while working in call centers that contribute to the overall decline in customer service. It is my hope that these "call center flashbacks" will serve as teachable moments and prompt readers to analyze their work ethic more closely. Please understand this book is coming from a genuine place, a passion for everyone to understand the value and need to exhibit a strong work ethic in all of our doings. When you think about it, we spend a significant amount of our lives in the workplace, so why should our time in the workplace be filled with frustration and despair? Why should this time be consumed with selfish actions that do not support the needs of the whole? I hope this book will encourage employees to shift their mind-set to make the workplace a more harmonious and successful environment.

Chapter 1

Why This Book?

Customer service is becoming a lost art. Most companies claim to embrace the customer service methodology through their mission statements and core values. If you were to browse through various company websites, you will see a reference about the customer and the importance of providing world-class service. But when *you*, the customer, interact with these companies, there tends to be a disparity between the established core values and the actual service being provided. So, where is the disconnect? What is causing customer service to falter? There are a plethora of reasons why we are seeing lackluster service and nonchalant actions from those who are hired to uphold their employers' values. Let's explore some factors that have caused a decline in overall customer service.

The Downsizing of America's Workforce

Downsizing is a common reaction to our economic woes and a desire for companies to make bigger profits. The bottom line is companies are now doing more with less. A vast number of employees have been downsized because of the reduction of the workforce, transferring functions offshore, or outsourcing customer service functions to other companies. All of these actions can impact a company's ability to provide proper service to its customer base. A reduction in the workforce can create inefficiencies in processes such as slower processing turnaround times and a lack of expertise and experience. Employees might feel pressed to work faster or cut corners to meet deadlines, which can result in costly errors and an increase in customer complaints. Typically, a wealth of experienced and knowledgeable employees is lost when a company makes the decision to downsize. Every company has that "go-to" person who knows what to do and whom to contact to get an issue resolved. When these valuable employees are downsized, that critical link in the organization's ability to resolve customer issues is weakened. Some companies have made decisions to transfer their functions to other countries for lower wages or higher tax write-offs. Because of these actions, customers are now faced with language barriers that can have a negative impact on customer service. Unfortunately, speaking with a customer service representative who has a very strong accent can be frustrating to some customers. These customers may not even give the representative a chance to resolve the issue, which is unfair to the customer service representative. On the other hand, some companies make the decision to outsource customer service functions to other businesses. Implications such as subpar training and the inability to execute functions in an efficient and accurate manner are becoming common-place. We also see that training departments are typically one of the first areas downsized or eliminated, which can result in "watered-down" or shortened training for the employees. As such, when an undertrained employee is placed in a position to represent his or her employer on the phone or in person, you can only imagine the dilemma the employee is faced with if he or she is not equipped to properly service the customer.

Employees: a Valuable Resource

One of the most valuable resources a company has is its employees. Employers have the responsibility to ensure their employees feel appreciated and are equipped for the job they do. In call centers, employees are basically on the phone for their entire shift because resolving customer inquiries is the basic expectation in this role. Granted, this is the job they were hired to perform, but because of the repetition of handling call after call and basically being tied to their work stations for extended periods, customer service representatives can become restless. Therefore, it is helpful to incorporate other responsibilities that can enrich their job, which increases their self-worth. If employees do not feel appreciated or are disengaged, performance drops and poor attendance can occur. (Years ago this was called *employee burnout*; the employee is weary of handling call after call with a good portion being from upset customers.) Disability-related absences might also increase because some employees will do what they can to take a break from work. Another important aspect is ensuring employees receive the proper tools to effectively perform their job. Companies must understand the importance of providing an excellent training foundation to their employees. When companies provide this kind of support, employees have a better sense of empowerment when serving their customers.

If employers have an unusually higher attrition or turnover rate, they must take the necessary steps to determine the root cause(s). Employees need to see and feel that senior management is connected with them and aware of the obstacles that prevent them from fully executing their roles. Employers should take the blinders off and reach out to their employees for suggestions and trends that can make their jobs more fulfilling. Employers cannot have the tunnel vision of profit only and neglect to significantly invest back into their employees.

An important task for supervisors is to determine why an employee has a performance problem. Historically, coaching models have suggested an employee's lacking performance could be related to either a "skill issue" or a "will issue." A skill issue indicates the performance could be improved through coaching or additional up-training. A will issue indicates the lacking performance is due to an attitude problem; this means the employee has the skills to perform the job, but he or she just doesn't want to perform the job. In addition to skill or will issues, I would also like to include another reason for subpar performance: the issue of "other ills." Other ills can be in the form of a sickness, substance abuse (such as drug or alcohol addictions), or even post-traumatic stress disorders that contribute to low performance.

To Incent or not to Incent? That is the Question.

You would think company incentives or bonus plans would be an acceptable way to compensate employees for high performance. In addition to their base pay, employees are rewarded for meeting certain stretch goals. What's not to like about that? If the incentive plan is soundly structured without any loopholes, it can be a valuable way to reward top performers. Conversely, if structured loosely and not properly monitored, the impact on customer service can be costly financially and brand-wise. Company incentives and bonuses can take the form of money, gift cards, or points to redeem for merchandise. In a call center environment, the incentive is usually based on employees' production (the number of phone calls employees handle or the number of sales they make), quality (how well employees adhere to established policies and procedures), and some form of attendance or schedule adherence. Typically, there are thresholds of performance; the better the performance, the higher the bonus. Now this is all well and good, but with the increase of productivity comes the need to have more resources dedicated to quality assurance. If the company does not increase its quality assurance efforts to match the rise in productivity, quality results can be skewed and give a false impression of *good quality*. On the dark side, employees might take the chance to eliminate required procedures in order to increase their productivity, thereby gaining a larger bonus. An incentive as such is likened to a dangling carrot—it can tempt employees to cut corners or not be as thorough in order to meet the qualifications for a bonus payout. I do believe loosely structured incentives, downsizing, and lack of integrity were contributing factors in our country's economic decline. If a manager's incentive payout is partly based on employees' performance, the manager might look the other way when employees are being unethical in dealings or finding loopholes to circumvent the process. Basically, all of this boils down to ethics!

The Burdens of Life

Life is becoming more complicated and stressful these days. People face problems away from the workplace and cannot focus on providing stellar customer service on the job. It can be difficult to separate from life issues when at work. Oftentimes, the pressures of life are distractors that can cause employees to make mistakes or incur a high number of absences. Life can also push employees to lose their composure with others and act in ways that are not businesslike. Financial woes have made it necessary for some of us to have multiple jobs in order to make ends meet. Juggling multiple jobs, family obligations, and other commitments can take a physical toll and lead to employees being less productive and focused while at work. Some people are working as much overtime as their companies will allow, but are they truly being productive and precise while working these grueling hours?

Health issues and other conditions can impact the effectiveness of employees' performance. Imagine the challenge to remain focused in providing excellent service when your body is in pain or you have received some disturbing health news. We are living in a day and age when sickness is prevalent but people still need to work in order to make ends meet. Some employees must work while taking medications that can have an adverse effect on how they execute their daily duties. Because they need their jobs and insurance benefits, some employees will press through their illnesses. As mentioned earlier, employees who suffer with some form of substance abuse have a difficult time remaining focused. The internal battle of soothing their addiction and properly serving their customers can present a daily challenge. Most companies understand the need to offer some type of employee assistance program where employees can seek confidential, professional help on a myriad of topics. It is in employees' best interest to take time to review the various company benefits available to them.

Other employees are not happy with their jobs and are not motivated to perform their best at work. Imagine how frustrating it can be if you feel you are in an unfulfilling job or you had to take a job in which the pay is not good and raises are few and far between. These burdens of life can make you feel discouraged. You might even catch yourself making comments such as, "They don't pay me enough!" or, "I'm just working here until I get a better job." Because some employees are not happy in the workplace, they will not work with a passion to satisfy the customer.

A Poor Work Ethic

Unfortunately, some employees have unsatisfactory work ethics, such as poor attendance, dishonesty, or not doing an honest day's work. When faced with such behaviors, it is a challenge for a company to establish a loyal base of satisfied customers. When a company allows poor attendance, the burden is placed on the other employees to pull the weight from those who did not report to work or report on time. Basically, a poor work ethic affects the customers as well as the employees. Dishonest employees who intentionally do not honor their commitments made to customers also have a negative impact on customer service. Customers become frustrated because of the extra time needed to follow up with an issue they were under the impression was already resolved. Imagine the concern when customers call to follow up only to find out no action was taken on their initial request. Some employees can view a poor work ethic in others and begin to adopt these behaviors if they feel management is not addressing such actions. Have you ever worked at a company with a specific negative culture? It is my opinion that the negative behaviors were tolerated over a period of time and other employees saw where they were not addressed, so they jumped on the bandwagon. The result: negative behaviors become rampant to the point that they become a culture or the norm in the workplace. If you were to have conversations with those who have worked at call centers, they can speak about call centers known for their negative culture. I have heard of call centers notorious for their unprofessional behavior, cutthroat management, or unethical activities—all of which were probably long-term behaviors that developed into a company culture. Note also that the workplace in some call centers has developed a positive culture due to the employer taking continual steps to remain engaged with the employees' needs.

After years of coaching, I came to the realization that some employees might struggle with displaying proper work ethics due to their upbringing. Honestly, some people don't do better because they don't know better. I recall a conversation with an employee about work ethics. This young lady had a strong work ethic—dependable and honest. She was telling me how her grandfather instilled positive influences in her family, which helped frame her strong work ethic. We began to discuss how some employees did not have positive role models during their formative years and, as a result, their work ethics might be underdeveloped. It was an eye-opening conversation to recognize and appreciate the positive influences we had in our lives. We also had employees who had positive role models but for whatever reason chose to adopt a poor work ethic. Of course I am not a psychologist, but I believe a strong or immature work ethic is developed through environment, life experiences, and the personal choices we make.

Chapter 2

Call Center Dynamics

A call center is a facility used for the purpose of receiving large volumes of calls or making high-volume outbound calls to customers or potential customers. The beauty of a call center is that calls are handled in a centralized location where call volume can be managed more efficiently. There are two types of call centers: inbound and outbound. Inbound call centers are for customers who need to contact the company for assistance such as technical help, status questions, or to place an order, while an outbound call center will have customer service representatives contact customers or potential customers. Outbound call centers are typically established for telemarketing or collection efforts and usually have more assertive employees as they are trying to sell a product or collect past due payments. Therefore, you probably will not encounter the best soft skills demonstrated in an outbound environment because the main focus is making a sale or collecting money. In this book, the customer service portion is mainly applicable to inbound call centers where customers have an established and vested relationship with the company and expect proper customer service in return. There can also be an inbound call center that services internal customers who work for the same company, probably from a different business unit. Whether internal or external customers, it is still customer service and the customer service representatives need to meet the same expectations of customer service excellence.

A typical call center has established service objectives regarding a time frame in which a call should be answered. For example, a service objective might be to answer 80 percent of incoming calls within twenty-five seconds. For call center services outsourced by businesses, financial penalties can come into play if the agreed-upon service objectives or performance guarantees are not met. Therefore, to ensure these objectives are obtained, the call center will have a workforce management team responsible for forecasting and monitoring call volume to ensure customer service representatives are efficiently handling calls. The workforce management team is a vital element in the success of a call center as it utilizes software and historical data to forecast call volume at any given time. The team will also take proactive steps to ensure the call center is sufficiently staffed to handle the call volume. This can be achieved by utilizing some type of break optimization process that determines the best time to have employees begin their shifts and when to take breaks and lunch. The workforce management team will also determine the need to offer overtime based on forecasted peak call volume. If call volume suddenly peaks for a sustained amount of time, it is common for workforce management to send out a communication soliciting for overtime or to reduce lunchtimes to the minimum amount. On the other hand, the workforce management team can reduce staff by offering voluntary time off during nonpeak hours. Voluntary time off is typically a win-win because employees can leave early without pay and employers can reduce their payroll costs.

Even though call centers service various products, the concepts of managing a call center are very similar, which makes it relatively easy for employees with call center experience to get jobs rather quickly. I'm sure you know of people who seem to get new jobs at call centers rather effortlessly. It's because they have the basic call center skills that will typically result in a minimal learning curve, which will make them more productive in a shorter period of time. The product might be different at call centers, but employees are expected to have good quality, productivity, and excellent customer service skills. Another key component in a call center is *adherence* (also known as *compliance* or *reliability*). Adherence determines how well each customer service representative adheres to his or her daily schedule. This is very important because employees are needed to be on the phone when they are scheduled to handle the call volume that workforce management forecasted. If they are not at their workstation taking calls, the possibility of missing service objectives increases. The expectation varies by call center, but the typical goal is somewhere in the 90 percent range. For example, if the call center's adherence goal is 94 percent, this would mean the representatives must adhere to their work schedule at least 94 percent of the time. Each representative has a daily schedule that outlines his or her work schedule such as start time, breaks, and lunchtime, as well as special activities such as meetings or training sessions. Because call volume can fluctuate rather quickly, schedules can change in an instant, so it is important for the representative to view his or her schedule throughout the day and adhere to it as closely as possible. During his or her scheduled phone time, the representative is expected to be on the phone taking calls; he or she should have very minimal interruptions from receiving calls. As such, if the schedule indicates a break, the representative should take a break as close to the scheduled time as possible. Let's circle back to the workforce management team. It determines the best time for representatives to take their breaks and lunch to ensure optimal service results.

Many of us have worked at a call center during our career. According to The United States Department of Labor, Bureau of Labor Statistics, there are well over two million customer service jobs in the United States with a projected growth of 12.6 percent by 2022. This means many more will work at a call center in the future, thereby creating a bigger need for call center awareness. Furthermore, demographic information reveals that most call center customer service jobs are currently in Texas, followed by Florida and California. What's common with these states is the year-round mild weather and the reduced likelihood of weather-related absences. The physical makeup of a call center is unique, and the size of call centers can range from small to substantially large groups. Visualize the following: you have a bunch of employees in an open space, sitting in cubicles with a telephone headset and computer on each desk. The desks are strategically placed to get the most workstations as possible. It can get rather loud in the call center because everyone is on phone calls serving their customers. An employee's workstation is separated by partitions to help buffer the noise levels. Some call centers are growing so fast that they must use desk sharing for their employees until they can obtain more space. These tight quarters can be visualized as sardines packed in a can—without the oil! An attractive option available to some call center employees is to work from home. The employees will need to have a designated work area at home and all that's needed is the necessary equipment such as a computer, phone, and a separate Internet connection. *Voila!* The employees can serve their customers in the luxury and comfort of their homes. A call center is a melting pot of personalities, cultures, experience, hormones, and work ethics that make life at a call center challenging and oftentimes comical.

Call centers are usually segmented by teams overseen by team supervisors. Team sizes can range from a few to twenty, and with the recent emphasis on working lean, supervisors are now managing teams on the higher end. The team supervisors coach each team member to meet established goals in areas such as production, quality, attendance, and adherence. Even though the team supervisors coach individual performance, overall team results are tracked as well. As with any team, the supervisors want to ensure their teams' performance is at its best. It is very common that team supervisors' overall team performance is factored in the supervisors' personal performance appraisals. This is one of many reasons supervisors want the best performance from their teams, as it is tied to their performance reviews.

Those who have not worked in a call center might believe this is an easy job. I beg to differ. Working in a call center as a customer service representative is a very demanding job. Some of the most important skills and expectations are outlined below.

Good Attendance and Timeliness

Especially at inbound call centers, there is no control over call volume because the customers are contacting the call center for assistance. As mentioned earlier, most call centers have service goals or answer rates, which confirms the importance of being available to answer calls in a timely manner. When customers call for assistance, we can't include an automated message saying, "Please excuse our heavy call volume at this time. We have forty employee callouts and twenty-eight are running late, so please call back at a later time." Poor attendance and timeliness can have a negative impact on the call center meeting service objectives. Because of this, attendance is strongly monitored in a call center. It boils down to basic facts: phone representatives must be present and on time to handle the incoming call volume. It is also important for the representatives to return from breaks and lunch on time. Unfortunately, a high percentage of terminations at a call center is the result of attendance violations.

Multitasking

A great way to increase productivity is to demonstrate multitasking skills throughout the call. Being able to notate the account or research policies while talking to the customer is a valuable skill that can shave valuable seconds off a phone call. The less time it takes to handle a call, the better the representative's productivity. Some people struggle in this area and cannot handle various duties simultaneously.

Good Typing Skills

Typing or data entry is required in a call center. In order to be as productive as possible, it is an advantage to have efficient and accurate typing skills. Keep in mind productivity is a critical performance objective, so if you are not efficient on the keyboard, you might have a slight disadvantage. In fact, some employers have some form of typing test to determine if the applicant would be a good fit. In addition to good typing skills, being able to efficiently work a computer is an advantage. Those customer service representatives who utilize hot keys instead of the standard mouse pointing, clicking, and dragging show a more efficient productivity.

Teamwork

Most call centers function in a team environment. Successful customer service representatives are flexible and willing to work with others. You have to learn to coexist in a call center and always remember your individual work is an integral part of a team's overall results. Teams in a call center can be likened to sports teams. Everyone has to contribute and do his or her best for the overall success of the team. I'm a huge NBA fan. It's very common to see team members encourage each other if someone is having a bad game. They will pull the team member aside and give some motivational talk or even give some in-the-moment coaching. You will even see them pat the team member on his backside—but keep in mind you can't pat someone on the backside in the workplace!

Quick Learner

Because call volume might be high, there are times when customer service representatives are not able to get off-line time to review updates to policies. In order to stay abreast of technical information, one must be a quick learner and able to multitask numerous duties.

Communication Skills and Professionalism

Employers have clear policies on customer service expectations. Being able to professionally communicate to your customers and remain personable are key factors that should be embraced. Customers expect to be treated with respect, and as the representative of your company, this is a top priority. A customer service representative can't allow his or her frustrations to manifest while speaking with customers. In addition, a representative must demonstrate sound communication skills and professionalism off the phones.

Patience and Empathy

Customers are diverse and interpret information differently. You cannot lose your patience if a customer needs you to repeat information or further clarify something. If a customer does not understand the information provided, a strong customer service representative will provide more details that will help the customer better interpret the information.

Thick Skin

We typically hear about unprofessional behavior by customer service representatives, which is a contributing factor of this book. I have, however, witnessed customers going over the deep end with vulgar name calling and profanity. Even though the customer might say something that is offensive, a customer service representative should not retaliate. The customer service representative should have a thick skin so he or she is not easily offended. This is not the environment to do a "tit for tat." However, you should not bear the brunt of such abuse. The typical policy is to notify your manager when a customer becomes abusive.

Call Control

A customer service representative must practice effective call control when interacting with customers. It is important not to allow the call to get off task as this can make the phone call longer, thereby making it difficult to meet production goals. The representative must have a healthy balance of efficiency and customer engagement. Too much customer engagement will negatively impact productivity. Too little engagement will negatively impact customer satisfaction scores. At times the representative might have a customer who needs extra clarity on a given topic. The representative should pick up on cues and ask probing questions to identify the customer's needs. There can also be a customer who has encountered a recent tragedy and might need someone to talk with, or the customer might just be lonely. Some customers require minimal assistance; they just want to get their issue resolved and end the call. Whatever the situation, the representative must be agile and adapt his or her service delivery to make the customer feel valued. The representative must also be able to practice efficiency while making the customer feel valued. Having that healthy balance between productivity and a great customer experience is a skillful aptitude. Engage with the customer to a certain extent, but know that you must strive to end the call so that you can move to the next customer. Representatives should utilize effective call control tactics when dealing with very talkative customers who want to hold extended conversations on unrelated topics. If the representative does not demonstrate effective call control, he or she will find it difficult to meet production expectations. I have seen extremes with call control; representatives can be overly accommodating to the customer, making their productivity too low. On the other hand, I have seen representatives who are so focused on productivity they do not engage with the customers and will rush them off the call.

Chapter 3

What Customers Say about Customer Service

Customers have a strong presence, and more than ever are voicing their feelings about the way they are being served. Customers can use numerous outlets to express their concerns and compliments. One of the most traditional formats is word of mouth, which is a powerful vehicle. In our modern age, customers have put a spin on word of mouth through the use of social media such as Facebook, Twitter, blogs, and even YouTube to share their customer experiences—both the good and the bad. Companies must be mindful of the power of social media. Because customers have so many avenues to voice their negative experiences, businesses must keep the concept of providing excellent customer service prevalent. It behooves a business to remain proactive and in tune with the pulse of its customers. By failing to do so, a business could find itself in a public campaign targeting its poor customer service. You can search the Internet for examples of poor customer service—it is rampant with companies that have trends with poor customer service. We are now seeing companies reach out to their customers by inviting them to take part in a survey after the phone call to share their customer service experience. This gives the customers the opportunity to provide feedback on the service they received from the customer service representative or the company. I hope this information is being reviewed and shared with the representatives; if a company is not using this feedback as a coaching tool, it is missing out on valuable customer input.

American Express is known for its strong focus on customer service and publishes a yearly survey that tracks the pulse of the consumer. The 2014 findings reveal consumers are rewarding great customer service more than ever. The U.S. findings in the 2014 American Express Global Customer Service Barometer revealed the following:

- 68 percent of consumers stated they would spend more money for excellent customer service.
- 29 percent of consumers believed that companies missed their customer service expectations.
- 38 percent of consumers believed that businesses pay less attention to providing good customer service (an increase from the previous year's results).
- Consumers will tell eight people when they have a good customer service experience and twenty-one people when they have a poor customer service experience.
- 60 percent of consumers intended to conduct business with a company but decided not to because of poor customer service.
- While most consumers are willing to give a company at least one or more chance after receiving poor customer service before they consider switching, 37 percent immediately considered switching after the initial poor customer service experience.

These are some revealing results that companies should share with their employees. Isn't it amazing to know how our actions in the workplace can retain customers or push them to take their services to a competitor? We should understand the impact of our actions in everything we do—at work and away from work.

"Good service is good business because it creates impassioned, loyal customers," said Kelly Fisher, Senior Vice President, Relationship Care Strategy, at American Express. "Those engaged customers spend more and share their excitement with others, which often influences their buying decisions. It's why willingness to recommend a product or company to a friend has become such an important measure for service companies. Service can really be a powerful way to drive the growth of a business."

Call center flashback: Recently my refrigerator needed repair, so the manufacturer recommended I contact a local business that services the brand of my refrigerator. I called and was immediately greeted by a representative who must have woken up on the wrong side of the bed. She came across as if my questions were silly and I was a bother. Mind you, this was the first time I had to get my refrigerator repaired so I might have had some elementary questions. Within one minute into the phone call I was already thinking about taking my business elsewhere, which I did. I advised the representative I would take my business elsewhere because she was not helpful. This company lost out on income as well as the possibility of referrals for future business. Customer service representatives are the front line to the company. Their excellent service can retain and grow business, or their poor service can drive it away.

Chapter 4

Call Center Phones

The phones used in call centers are specifically designed for handling calls in a high-volume environment. The phones have all the bells and whistles that help customer service representatives provide an efficient and customer-focused experience. The call center phone system is programmed to include its own network of frequently used contact numbers and speed dial options—all of which helps make the phone call with the customer more efficient. It's all about the time factor in a call center, and the phone system will serve as that tool. We'll review the components of call center phones more in detail along with their proper use, as well as review the crafty and unethical ways *some* representatives use the phones for personal or selfish motives. Throughout this book, real-life scenarios of inappropriate employee behavior will be shared. In line with the classic television show *Dragnet*, please be advised of the following disclaimer with a slight spin: The story you about to "hear" is true. The names have been changed to protect the "guilty"! In all fairness, I will also share some positive call center flashbacks that confirm some employees take their responsibilities seriously.

Auto-in/ready

This is the state that allows customer service representatives to receive incoming calls. At the beginning of their shifts, customer service representatives will log on the phone with their assigned ID numbers. This is key, as this personal ID number tracks their individual actions and performance. Time and service are of the essence at a call center. After representatives log on to the computer and phone they are to press the "auto-in/ready" button to begin receiving calls. Until they press "auto-in/ready," calls will not be routed to them; they will remain in an idle state typically referred to as *default aux*. This phone state of default aux is acceptable at the beginning of the shift to allow the representatives to pull up their various systems. Once all of their systems/databases are open, they are to begin receiving calls. The phone state of default aux can be an area of abuse as some employees will take an unusually long time before they press "auto-in/ready" to begin receiving calls. I have seen representatives log on the phone and remain in default aux to visit their friends, go to the restroom, or get a snack—even when calls are in queue! (Calls in queue means customers are waiting for their calls to be answered.)

Hold

At times, a customer service representative might need to place a customer on hold to review account history or get assistance. Most companies have required time frames as to how long a customer should be placed on hold. Call center etiquette typically dictates the representative should get permission from the customer before placing him or her on hold and the representative should provide the customer an estimate of the hold time. A common industry standard is to keep a customer on hold for no longer than two minutes. While a customer is on hold the representative should focus on resolving the issue for which the customer was placed on hold. The representative should not get sidetracked with personal agendas such as talking to coworkers, reading text messages, or hoping the customer will get tired of waiting and hang up.

Call center flashback: In typical call centers, managers have access to view the phone states of all employees. The various reports show if the representative is on a call, the length of the call, and if the representative is not available to receive incoming calls. On this particular day, I was monitoring phone activity and noticed Juan's phone state was showing he had his customer on hold for more than four minutes and he was not at his desk. A four-minute hold time far exceeded this company's established time frame, so I began to look for Juan to make sure he returned to his customer. I checked to see if he was getting help from one of our subject matter experts, but he could not be located. While walking past the breakroom (yes, the breakroom) I noticed Juan was popping popcorn in the microwave! Now, how inconsiderate was that? I'm sure the customer thought Juan was performing account-related activities, not getting something to eat. Needless to say, this questionable action resulted in a write-up in his file.

Transfer

This option is used when a customer service representative needs to transfer the customer to a specific individual or another department. Phone etiquette would require the representative to advise the customer where the call is being transferred. There are two types of transfers, and a company's phone-handling policy dictates which method is considered appropriate. The first is a warm transfer in which the representative transfers the call but remains on the line until the receiving party answers in order to give the receiver some details about the call. The advantage of a warm transfer is that the original representative the customer spoke with will take the initiative to share details as to why the call is being transferred. It basically keeps the customer from explaining the whole scenario over again, which can be a frustrating situation.

The other transfer is a cold transfer. A cold transfer occurs when the representative transfers a call to another person or department, but in this case the representative just reroutes the call; he or she does not remain on the line to introduce the call to the receiving party. This type of transfer is usually performed when the customer needs assistance from a totally unrelated department or in the case of misrouted calls. Note the transfer button is not intended to transfer a customer to another department just because the representative does not want to help the customer.

Call center flashback: I received a call from a customer with a complaint on customer service representative Sarah. The customer said Sarah was rude and was unwilling to help resolve her issue. Actually, when I heard the customer's feedback about Sarah, I was not shocked. Sarah had a history of questionable phone actions such as placing customers on hold for extended periods and speaking to customers in a curt/unhelpful manner. The customer was able to provide the date and time of the call, which was enough information for me to locate and listen to the recorded call. While listening to the recorded call, I noticed Sarah was indeed not demonstrating a willingness to help, so the customer asked to speak to a supervisor. Sarah began to recite company policies almost robotically, which further frustrated the customer. At this time, the customer became adamant about speaking with a supervisor, and, mind you, several supervisors were available during this time, including myself. Instead of allowing the customer to speak to a supervisor, Sarah cold transferred the customer to another department in hopes the customer would get lost in the deep abyss of misrouted calls. What Sarah did not count on was a persistent customer who had had enough and wanted to make sure Sarah received the necessary feedback on her poor performance. The odd thing is, Sarah was a delightful young lady when she was not on the phones. Our individual meetings were always pleasant and she appeared receptive to feedback. It just seems that taking phone calls was a stressful situation for her. This is why it is so important to find the job or career in which you can flourish and not feel stifled. Because Sarah had an established pattern of this behavior, it was easy to document her performance and recommend corrective action.

Mute

The mute button silences the call and prevents the customer from hearing the representative. The appropriate use of the mute button is to prevent the customer from hearing a cough or sneeze, or in instances of on-the-job training when the representative is being coached during the call. Unfortunately, some representatives have adopted the mute button as an option to spew outbursts of frustration and sarcasm toward the caller. A common outburst heard on the floor is "get off my phone!" or "this customer is getting on my nerves!" I have also heard profanity and banging on desks. A true word of caution: customer service representatives thought they pressed the mute button to vent only to find the customer actually heard them rant and rave. The thing about inappropriate muting is that other representatives tend to adopt the negative behavior. If this behavior is not nipped in the bud, you will see this behavior permeate the call center, thereby becoming a company culture. When advocates see others doing something without repercussion, others may think they can do the same thing.

After Call Work (ACW)

A representative uses this state to complete call-related activities after ending a call with a customer. Once the call-related activities are complete the representative should press "auto-in/ready" to take the next call. As long as the representative remains in ACW, he or she will not receive another call, so it is critical for managers to ensure representatives are wrapping up calls in the most efficient manner possible. Keep in mind the time spent in ACW is factored in the total productivity time. Basically the more calls you take in a day, the better your productivity. Various behaviors can extend time in ACW:

1. **The Avoider**: Some representatives will delay their wrap-up (ACW) activities in order to delay taking the next call. They will implement inefficient activities that appear to be valid actions, but if you really focus on what they are doing, you will see it is unnecessary busy work.

2. **The Breather**: This representative needs to decompress after calls. It is understandable to take a breather in ACW after a tense and difficult call because you don't want to take that negative energy into the next call. However, some representatives take breathers in ACW on the majority of their calls, which negatively impacts their overall productivity.

3. **The Commentator**: This representative wants to share the details of the call with coworkers. Such play-by-play recaps only add valuable seconds to total handle time and slows productivity. This can have multiple impacts because the Commentator is also disrupting coworkers' ability to efficiently handle their calls.

4. **Skill deficiency**: Some representatives work as hard and fast as they can but are not efficient with their wrap-up activities. The opportunity is to pinpoint the skill that needs to be enhanced in order to improve overall productivity. Monitoring representatives' actions in real time can reveal developmental opportunities. A common skill deficiency is not being able to multitask—to talk and type at the same time.

5. **No sense of urgency**: Some representatives have the ability to efficiently complete their call-related activities and move to the next call, but they have a "will" issue, which was discussed in chapter 1. They just don't want to do the job because of workplace immaturity.

Call center flashback: Florence was known as having one of the lowest productivity results in the call center. She recently moved to my team and I noticed her talk time (amount of time spent assisting the customer on the phone) was very good, but her ACW was extremely high. Her quality was also very good, which would suggest Florence had sufficient skills to handle her calls. I had to determine why Florence's ACW was so high. What was she doing in ACW that prevented her from moving on to take another phone call? During initial coaching sessions, she did not give a reason for having such a high ACW. I reminded her of the need to lower her ACW in order to improve her overall productivity results. On one particular day, I informed Florence I would be sitting with her to monitor her performance. I advised that I was just taking notes and she was to handle her calls as if I was not present. While sitting with Florence, I noticed she was very knowledgeable of policies and efficient in navigating through the various systems. She was a fast typist and could multitask well. She handled her calls effortlessly and moved to the next call quickly. I was impressed! But still, why was Florence's ACW historically high? Upon completing the monitoring session, I returned to my desk to write up my analysis. I pulled several summary interval reports from previous days and compared them to the summary interval report during the time I sat with Florence. Note: Summary interval reports are historical reports that show the number of calls handled by a representative and the amount of time used in states such as ACW and hold. Upon review of the reports, I noticed Florence's productivity during the hour I sat with her was much higher than during the intervals when I did not sit with her. I also noticed her ACW was much lower during the interval I sat with her, so again the question was what was causing Florence to have such a high ACW when the supervisor was not sitting with her. Was she talking to her coworkers? Was she taking breathers between calls? Was she leaving her desk to talk to her coworkers while in ACW? Or was it all of these? I met with Florence to share my findings that she was very productive when I sat with her. I then shared the summary interval reports of her performance when I did not sit with her. When I asked why her ACW was so much higher when I did not sit with her, she admittedly said, "You busted me." Florence revealed she tends to take a breather after calls or might visit her coworkers when she is in ACW. After this coaching session, Florence began to show improvement with her ACW; however, she still required monitoring because of her workplace immaturity. Sometimes this statement is true: "When the cat's away, the mice will play."

I did the same exercise with Jake, another customer service representative at a different company. Jake was considered a subject matter expert; he was the go-to person regarding policies and various systems. He had the same pattern as Florence—an efficient talk time but a very high ACW—so I performed side-by-sides with Jake just to monitor his activities. I advised Jake the same thing I had told Florence: just work as normal, no need to have any dialogue with me. After performing the side-by-sides and review of the summary reports, it was confirmed Jake did not use a high amount of ACW when I sat with him. When I shared my findings with Jake, instead of taking ownership, he said I just happened to sit with him when he received easy calls. He said I was good luck because I brought easy calls his way. I beg to differ; Jake had been in this department for several years and consistently had low productivity. Needless to say, I performed the exercise about a month later and it revealed Jake's productivity was very high during the time I sat with him. The reality is that Jake should better manage his non-work activities during ACW so that he can move to take the next call.

Other Phone States

Customer service representatives will use other phone states to identify their current status.

Training: This state is used to identify those customer service representatives in some type of formal or informal training. Ideally this state should be preapproved; the representative should not use this state whenever they want to.

Meeting: A representative in this state is in a meeting of some sort, possibly a team meeting or individual meeting. This state should also be preapproved.

Special project: This can be considered a catch-all state to include time to research accounts, work on a special assignment, or help with a company event. The representative should obtain approval before going into this state.

System outage: At times the customer service representative will encounter system issues that prevent him or her from performing his or her duties. This state will identify the representative as someone experiencing system problems. In addition to acknowledging the system issue, the representative should be actively resolving the system issue. I have seen instances when a representative was in system outage but was not trying to fix the problem. The representative was milking the outage by taking extra time to visit coworkers or take a break off the phones.

Break: As mentioned previously, labor laws dictate the length and frequency of breaks that representatives must receive. These breaks appear on the representatives' daily schedules so they are not required to obtain prior approval. Their only expectation is to take their break as close to the assigned time as possible and to return to their workstations on time.

One major management issue is to minimize unwarranted activities in nonproductive states and to identify and rectify unintentional errors with phone states. An example of unintentional errors would be a representative going to break or lunch while in ACW. There are also times when representatives may leave for the day without logging off the phones. These types of errors can be readily identified through the active monitoring of various phone reports. Keep in mind, any time in ACW negatively impacts representatives' productivity, so it is to everyone's benefit to make sure these states are actively monitored. In tandem with monitoring reports, these states give an overall snapshot of the various activities occurring in a call center. You can access a real-time report and view the states/activities of each representative. Whether on a call, in

ACW, break, or special project, the report shows this detail as well as the amount of time in that state.

Instead of focusing on work-related activities, some representatives have been known to have in-depth, personal conversations with coworkers, eat meals at their desk, or just walk the floor visiting coworkers. This is why the workforce management team is so vital in maintaining a productive and efficient workforce. The workforce management team or other assigned personnel will monitor call states and reach out to the representative or supervisor to determine what the delay is.

Release button: This button is used to disconnect the line when the call has mutually ended between the customer service representative and the customer. On the dark side, this option is used to hang up on a customer who has not been completely served. Some representatives will press the release button for an incoming call or will allow a call to come through but not greet the customer in hopes the customer will hang up. Either way, these actions can increase representatives' productivity unethically.

Call center flashback: Randall's phone productivity was exceeding expectations. This was all good, but the fact that Randall was a new hire raised a red flag. How could someone who'd just learned the job have such outstanding productivity results? I have seen some new-hire representatives quickly move through the learning curve, but this is a rarity. Upon further review of his calls, it was noticed that Randall was disconnecting a portion of his calls by pressing the release button soon after he greeted the customer. This unethical activity made his productivity appear very high, but keep in mind he was not fully serving the customer. So the inconvenienced customer had to call back. Nothing much to be said here—Randall was terminated for this behavior.

Representatives can intentionally misuse their phone in various ways to avoid taking calls; this is referred to as phone manipulation or call avoidance. Representatives are assigned various skill sets based on their knowledge and training. A representative should receive the next call in his or her skill set as long as he or she remains in an available state. If the representative is in an available state waiting for a call and puts himself or herself in a non-available state (for even just one second) such as ACW, meeting aux, or default aux, the phone system will basically move the representative's next call position to the bottom of the queue, thereby delaying the time for him or her to receive the next call. This continued practice will prevent the normal flow of incoming calls and the representative will basically service fewer calls, hence call avoidance. Is this fair for the representative who is doing the right thing? No, it's not fair; if an occupancy report is pulled, you will see the employee who is avoiding calls has a lower occupancy rate, meaning they are receiving fewer calls to service.

Chapter 5

Consider Your Ways

Those who know me know I love music and am always coming up with a song for any situation. This chapter makes me think of Michael Jackson's song "Man in the Mirror." We need to look at the man or woman in the mirror and *"make that change."* When I was working for Prudential as a dental claims examiner, I was aiming to get promoted to the next level. In order to do this, I had to meet the established metrics for three consecutive months. I think I was placing too much pressure on myself because I would get close but miss quality for the month. I had a cassette tape (yes, I said cassette tape) of The Commodores with the song "Zoom" that I began to play each morning on the way to work. For some reason, this song put me in a zone that removed stress and frustrations; it's my healing song. To this day, I share this story with team members who are going through stressful moments at work. But I digress; let's get back to the topic of this chapter!

Do you know someone who seems to have so much drama in their work life or personal life? Granted, life itself brings challenges and situations we must navigate through, but there are times when we make life harder by the choices we make. Sometimes, we have to sit down in a quiet space, look in the mirror, and "consider our ways." We must be honest and ask ourselves these questions: Could the dilemmas I am experiencing at work be the result of my own actions? Do I have a poor attitude? Have I been involved in some questionable activities at work? Do I have consistent attendance issues resulting in corrective action write-ups? There are times when we must take an assessment of our actions and be honest with our circumstances. Let's take a quick self-assessment by answering yes or no to the following statements. You must genuinely be transparent and reflective on your various work experiences for you to have true findings.

1. Compared to coworkers, do you have a higher amount of customers requesting to speak with your supervisor because of poor service or unprofessionalism?

2. Have customers made comments that you are not helpful or have a negative attitude?

3. When on the phone with a customer, are you easily sidetracked with non-work distractions instead of remaining focused on the customer? (Non-work distractions can include reading books, talking to coworkers, checking text messages, primping in the mirror.)

4. Do you allow customers to frustrate you and press the mute button to vent?

5. Do you justify your actions when receiving feedback on complaints? (i.e., "Well, the customer was rude to me, and I was not going to allow someone to talk to me like that." Or, "I always get the crazy calls!")

6. Instead of making an effort to help your customers, do you voluntarily escalate calls to your supervisor/manager? (i.e. "Do you want to talk to my manager?")

7. Do your coworkers laugh and joke about the nonchalant way you serve your customers?

8. Even though you might be a source of information, do you find that coworkers are hesitant to approach you for help?

9. Do you have a history of complaints about your customer service skills? (Consider your previous jobs as well.)

10. Do your performance appraisals or quality audits speak about lacking soft skills?

I hope these questions will be an eye opener and help you realize there might be some opportunities to develop your customer service skills. The goal of this exercise is to help accept accountability for your actions, which will better prepare you for further greatness in this world. Keep in mind that customer service is a combination of people skills, communication, and ownership, which are transferrable skills in any job.

If you did not answer "yes" on any question, you have a strong customer service foundation and can successfully engage with your customers. Customers are usually pleased with your service.

If you answered "yes" to one question, there might be a red flag that needs to be addressed in one area. But still, you have strong customer service skills.

If you answered "yes" to two or three questions, there are some behaviors causing a disconnection between you and your customers and coworkers. Please take some time to seriously consider your ways.

If you answered "yes" to at least four questions, you are more than likely a distraction to others at work and immediate focus is highly recommended. Your actions are negatively impacting your individual and team results.

Chapter 6

Customer Service Basic Attributes (IPAD)

The previous chapter's self-assessment revealed your customer service aptitude. Based on your results, you might need to make some minor adjustments or a major overhaul. Whether in a call center or other customer service position, the employee must have some basic attributes in order to succeed in the workplace. I like to refer to these primary attributes as **IPAD**:

Integrity
Professionalism
Attitude
Dependability

Integrity

Webster's Dictionary defines integrity, in part, as "moral soundness; honesty; freedom from corrupting influence or motive." Basically, integrity is doing the right thing when one is seen and not seen. Let's be honest: some people have strong integrity and can be counted on to do the right thing while others have questionable ethics and will look for ways to circumvent a process for selfish reasons. An employee with high integrity is a valuable asset as he or she will strive to represent himself or herself and his or her employer in an honest and upright manner. When I had someone on my team with high integrity, I felt very fortunate because I could count on that person to adhere to policies and procedures. Sadly, when

I had someone on my team with questionable integrity, it was an internal battle to believe anything he or she said. It's likened to a parent when a child has broken the trust bond; the parent wants to believe the child, but the child's prior behaviors cause an internal battle of doubt. Employers are now offering comprehensive benefit packages that attract and help retain employees. Some parts of a comprehensive benefit package include health insurance, disability insurance, retirement plans, and paid time off, which includes bereavement. Employees should remember not to misuse company benefits as this could result in being placed under the umbrella of suspicion or even termination of employment. Sadly, the bereavement policy has turned out to be a top area of abuse, especially if the employer has a liberal policy. Bereavement policies will usually grant an employee paid time off to grieve the death of a family member. Common bereavement policies will grant up to three days off with pay and possibly more if the employee has to travel out of town. I have worked at companies with specific, clear-cut guidelines that define when an employee is eligible for bereavement. I have also seen where the employer implemented a generous policy that backfired because some employees viewed this as an opportunity to take time off work, with pay. A liberal policy might not closely define the eligible family member or place a limit on the number of bereavement absences employees may receive. Some employees will show questionable integrity by finding loopholes just to be able to take time off from work. There have been instances when some employees claimed bereavement an excessive number of times, which resulted in an investigation of their claims' validity. This is where an employee's level of integrity is questioned. I'm sure a liberal bereavement policy was implemented in good faith so employees would be able to customize their need for time off based on their relationship with the deceased. We have seen employees take the full allotted time off when they barely had a relationship with the deceased.

Earlier in this book, we discussed the concept of employer incentives being used to increase employee performance. Even though the intent is to produce higher results, some employees lose sight of integrity in order to earn an incentive payout. This example is clearly an issue of integrity.

Call center flashback: As with most call centers, Arnold was a customer service representative. His employer rolled out an incentive plan in which employees could earn a bonus payout for meeting specific performance goals. As with most incentive plans, the performance goals were designed to be challenging and require employees to stretch themselves in order to earn a bonus. The higher the performance, the better the payout. Arnold was so thrilled to have a chance to supplement his income with the possibility of earning more money each month. During the first few months, Arnold was not able to receive the bonus because he was just shy of meeting the production portion of the incentive plan. Arnold became frustrated with the fact that he was missing out on the bonus and noticed other employees were earning bonuses each month. So one day Arnold began to disconnect a few incoming calls here and there. He also began to unnecessarily transfer some calls to other departments, all in an effort to enhance his productivity. As a result, Arnold met the production stretch goal and earned the bonus. Arnold was hooked! Each month he did some type of phone manipulation in order to earn a bonus. Eventually, the quality department monitored one of Arnold's calls in which he disconnected the call. This led to an investigation of his calls, during which a pattern of abuse was noticed. Because phone manipulation is considered gross misconduct, Arnold was soon terminated from the company. Unfortunately, Arnold's integrity was compromised and he forgot about a key component of his job: providing excellent service to his customers. Because he wanted to make bonus, he committed some unethical actions that led to the termination of his employment.

Professionalism

Professionalism can be described as displaying appropriate conduct, skills, or appearance in the workplace. Presenting a high level of professionalism is vital for employees because their actions are a direct reflection of the company. As for customer service representatives, they are typically the first point of contact for a customer, so it is critical to present that great first impression. Let's explore some specific actions that will ensure professionalism in the workplace.

Communication: The following are some commonsense "must dos" in the workplace:

- Avoid slang and profanity in the workplace.
- Be sure to speak with good diction and grammar.
- Ensure your writing skills are both professional and clear.
- Empathize when appropriate. Sometimes customers want to hear a sincere apology.

- Use positive words and a sincere tone when interacting with your customers.

Positive words and courtesy phrases are used to enhance the customer experience and help create a professional image. Examples include:

- **I will be glad** to handle that for you.
- **It has been a pleasure** serving you today.
- **Thank you**.
- **Please**.
- **No problem**.
- **May I have** that number?
- **I understand** that can be frustrating.

If you find it difficult to include such language when communicating with your customers, try to incorporate positive words in your personal life until it becomes a habit. It is documented that it takes twenty-one days for something to become a habit. I previously implemented a "Twenty-One-Day Positive Word Challenge" in which the team was encouraged to use positive words during non-phone and personal conversations. The goal was to use teamwork and repetition to help others remember to include positive words in regular conversations. If a person missed an opportunity to use positive words, the team member would remind him or her to rephrase the statement. This exercise helped the employees use positive words during their calls with customers because of repetition and practice.

Having a sincere and engaged tone is necessary for a successful customer service interaction. A phone interaction heavily depends on the sense of hearing how the customer feels. The customer cannot see the representative, so he or she will pick up on the representative's tone and sincerity. There can be a level of subjectivity on the part of the customer, but that's why it is important the representative portrays a sincere and engaged tone. When a customer is frustrated or upset, tone and sincerity are even more weighted in the view of the customer. Individuals who speak with a flat tone and no voice inflection can come across as nonchalant or unconcerned about the customer's issue. If a customer perceives that you are not helpful or sincere, he or she will not want to continue speaking with you, which could lead to a complaint. A significant percentage of complaints in a call center is not necessarily what the representative said but "how" he or she said it.

We should be mindful of our actions with customers as well as with coworkers. An issue with a customer or a coworker can agitate you to the third degree, so having a good level of restraint can prevent issues from escalating out of control. The late Flip Wilson used to say, "the devil made me do it!" Truly, we are ultimately responsible for our responses; we can't point blame and get easily provoked. Reality shows have taken over the airways like gangbusters. Even though they are called reality shows, they are far from real life and such outlandish behaviors should not be emulated in the workplace. Most characters on these shows are trying to bring a "shock value" that will make them "relevant" and guarantee another season or other lucrative opportunities. Using reality shows as a blueprint for workplace behavior is unrealistic and highly discouraged. You don't want to bring shock value to the workplace, and remember, you want to be relevant in a positive light. The majority of reality shows are laced with profanity, fights, arguments, and deception. So the next time you face conflict at work, please do not use a clip from your favorite reality show in response to a conflict. Now, don't get me wrong—I watch my share of reality shows, but it's for *entertainment purposes only!*

For customer service employees in a face-to-face relationship with their customers, professional appearance is very important. Make sure your dress is at least in line with your employer's established dress code. Clothes and appearance should be neat, clean, and not too trendy (unless you work in an environment where trendy is the product). Company dress codes are established to support a professional environment and to minimize distractions in the workplace. Employees should be sure to review the company's dress code policy to ensure their dress is in compliance. If your conscience says your dress is not appropriate, it's best to go with your conscience. Most company guidelines state employees might be sent home without pay if they are in violation of dress code policy. Because there are so many styles for females, we have the most dress code violations at work. Please remember to take an honest look in the mirror to see if there are any plunging neck lines or tight-fitting clothes that can cause a distraction to others. As someone who has recently put on a few pounds, I have found wearing long cardigan vests are a great way to cover your "assets"! It is also a good idea to dress for the role you aspire to. If you want to be promoted to a specific position, it's best to look the part in your current role. This shows you can represent the company with a professional image. Believe me: your appearance speaks volumes. If you report to work with a sloppy and slothful appearance, do you think your employer can envision you in a role of responsibility?

Some people like to chew gum and can handle it with modesty while others like to chew gum and advertise it to the world! Popping gum at work is unprofessional, but popping gum while you are talking to customers is even worse. At times, it seems as if employees are not aware of how hard they are chewing their gum because they are so focused on the task at hand. This is why it is not a good idea to chew gum at work if you cannot handle it with modesty. When I see people popping gum at work and in public, I think about Tyler Perry's movie *Medea's Family Reunion,* where Medea, Tyler Perry's character, was on the way home with a court-assigned, teenaged foster child. The teenager was being disrespectful and popping gum in the presence of an aggravated Medea. She had it! Medea yelled out to the teenager, "Little girl, if you don't stop poppin' that gum!" Well, the teenager continued her disrespectful act, which prompted Medea to give her a good ol' spanking in the backseat of the car.

Call center flashback: I was performing a side-by-side with a customer service representative during my first week of employment at a call center just to get insight on the type of calls received. The representative was very knowledgeable and efficient, but I noticed she would chew and pop her gum rather hard, and she wasn't even aware of it. It was so distracting that I could not even concentrate on the content of the phone call. All I could think about was Medea saying, "If you don't stop 'poppin' that gum!" At the end of our session, she asked me how she did. I told her I could not speak about the technical portion because I had not gone through any training yet, but I had to let her know the gum popping was not a good look.

Call center flashback: Deborah was a seasoned representative who had worked in the industry for several years. She came to my team with a history of poor customer service skills. She was knowledgeable in the technical arena but lacking in soft skills and professionalism. As long as the customer was calm and noncritical of her, Deborah's calls went fairly well. When the customer questioned her responses or expressed frustration with her, she would become combative, loud, and disruptive on the floor. What Deborah did not understand was that she was responsible for her responses to her customers. There is no place for a tit-for-tat mentality in the workplace; it is important to demonstrate workplace maturity. Her rants were a disturbance to others, most coworkers were hesitant to interact with her, and the supervisor had to continually address her performance issues, which took away time to equally focus on other team members. Deborah received regular coaching, but unfortunately was not able to show consistent improvement; as a result, she was placed on corrective action. Deborah eventually submitted her resignation, citing the job was not a good fit for her. Truth be told, I was relieved!

I'm not sure what field of work Deborah is in now, but I sincerely hope she has taken ownership of her behavior.

Cell phones. A world-changing piece of technology that offers convenience and the ability to remain connected with family, friends, and society. Users can handle their business and personal calls in almost any location. Before cell phones, you had to use a land line, such as a home/business phone or a phone booth, to contact others. Back in the day, if you wanted to meet up with friends you would agree to meet at a specific landmark at a specific time. With cell phones, you can make last-minute changes relatively easily and remain connected with your party. Society is attached to cell phones and social media; there is a gravitating need to respond or send messages in real time. On the other hand, cell phones in the workplace have been known to impede productivity, quality, and integrity. Initially, cell phones were large and not easy to conceal. Now everybody has a cell phone that is sleek, small, and silent! Cell phone use during work time has been such an issue that company policies have been amended to include specific verbiage on the proper use of cell phones. Company policies normally state cell phones can't be used in work areas for two reasons:

1. Most phones have electronic data capabilities where the user can text or take a picture of a customer's confidential information, such as credit card account numbers.

2. Using a cell phone while serving a customer can negatively affect quality and it lowers productivity.

There have been numerous breaches of cell phone use in the call center. Employees will place their cell phones in their drawers and periodically check social media or text messages. They will have them in their laps, which is typically unseen because they are seated at their desks. I have even seen representatives using their cell phones while they are talking to their customers. Even though the customers do not see this action, it comes across with delayed responses or having to ask the customers to repeat themselves because representatives were focused on their cell phones. Oddly, employees can get upset when the supervisor asks them to put away their phones. Keep in mind that the supervisor has to enforce the policy to ensure the best quality and productivity possible, but also to keep cell phone use from spreading in the workplace. If management allows it to be used by a few, then others will begin to use it—the result is that the vast majority are now using their cell phones instead of focusing on the customer or work at hand.

Call center flashback: Cell phone use in an actual face-to-face customer service environment is more noticeable than during a call center interaction. This particular flashback was not in an actual call center environment but a hospital emergency room. I was at the emergency room with my mother when a young lady called us for registration. Even though my mother's situation was not a dire emergency, you would still expect the representative to focus on the patient and issue at hand. The representative was obtaining insurance information from my mother and entering the information in the database when I noticed her stop and pull out her cell phone from her lap to read a message. The nerve of her! I did not say anything to her, but when we made eye contact, I looked at her cell phone in a silent attempt to let her know this is unacceptable behavior. She then put her cell phone back and resumed the registration process. For those who feel the need to be totally tied to your cell phone during work hours, you need some type of intervention. Please understand the perception that is tied to this behavior. Also understand how this behavior reduces your focus on the customer or job at hand; it comes across that the cell phone is the more important task, not the customer. Now, at times people need to be readily available because of life issues. This is when employees should communicate their need to a supervisor so that accommodations can be made.

Attitude

Many quotes from a variety of well-known sources address the importance of a good attitude. Here are some of the ones I like in particular:

> "People may hear your words but they feel your attitude." – *John C. Maxwell*

> "Your attitude, not your aptitude, will determine your altitude." – *Zig Ziglar*

> "Weakness of attitude becomes weakness of character." – *Albert Einstein*

> "Excellence is not a skill, it's an attitude." – *Ralph Marston*

> "A cheerful heart is good medicine, but a crushed spirit dries up the bones." – *Proverbs 17:22*

> "Choosing to be positive and having a grateful attitude is going to determine how you're going to live your life." – *Joel Osteen*

> "If you don't set a baseline standard for what you accept in life, you'll find it's easy to slip into behaviors and attitudes or a quality of life that is far below what you deserve." – *Tony Robbins*

> "Bad attitudes will ruin your team." – *Terry Bradshaw*

> "This you know, my beloved brethren, but everyone must be quick to hear, slow to speak, and slow to anger." – *James 1:19*

> "Your attitude is like a price tag. It shows how valuable you are." – *Unknown*

"A bad attitude is like a flat tire. You can't go anywhere until you change it." – *Unknown*

"Attitude is a little thing that makes a big difference." – *Winston Churchill*

"A positive attitude is not a destination, it's a way of life." – *Unknown*

And these are just a few statements on the importance of a positive attitude. It is vital to have a positive attitude in the workplace. Even if your job is not where you want to be, you should still strive to maintain a positive attitude. I'm sure you have heard the following remarks from coworkers or even found yourself saying such:

"Why should I work hard? The company does not appreciate me!"

"I'm just here until I get a better job!"

"They don't pay me enough to do all that!"

"I can't stand this job!"

"They never ask me to help with projects. That's why I don't care!"

Granted, this might not be your dream job, but it is the job you have now. So many people wish they had a job. When you catch yourself going down this slippery slope, you need some type of intervention, such as positive thinking or just being thankful that you have a job. Do what you need to do to stay positive; find a mentor, pray, or meditate. Remember this: you can always learn something from any job, so try to focus on the positive aspects of the job until you get your breakthrough. I get it, sometimes our employer fails us, but the customer should not be penalized with poor customer service because we have issues with our jobs. Until you find another job, be sure to maintain a good attitude. I recall a conversation with a representative where I was complimenting her great performance and attitude. As a new supervisor to the company, I was assigned to observe how she handled her calls—she was phenomenal with her customers and her craft. She shared with me that she had a poor attitude before I came to the company. She admitted she was a complainer and was a difficult person to work with and manage until she began to get tired of that behavior. She got tired of being difficult and wanted to be better. She took ownership of her situation. This young lady had an epiphany and she took the necessary steps to "make that change." With consistent focus, she made this change, management began to notice how well she evolved, and eventually she successfully posted and was selected for a new position. She began to remove herself from the call center drama; if someone brought negativity her way, she put a positive spin on it. This young lady developed her workplace maturity. But remember this is a process; management might not have a change of heart overnight. They want to see consistency with your change. I tell you, attitude is the key!

I have had coaching sessions with many people only to find they are not happy in their jobs. My response would be that it is OK to want another job, but while you are at your current job you need to do your best where you are until you find another job. Don't allow your frustrations to fester and lead to further negative behaviors such as poor attendance and subpar performance. There is one thing people tend to forget when they apply for an internal position with their current employer. Your performance is documented and readily available to the department you are applying to. This is why it is so important to maintain a positive attitude and strive to have the best performance possible. You want to be ready when the opportunity presents itself! T. D. Jakes said it best: "Get ready, get ready, get ready, get ready!"

Call center flashback: William was not happy in his current position as a customer service representative. He allowed his discontent with the job to spill over to his performance. His productivity was mediocre and he had high After Call Work (ACW) and low adherence. (Adherence in a call center measures your ability to adhere to your phone schedule.) William applied for a job in another department within his company and, as part of the application process, his previous performance results in his current role were provided to the department he applied for. I advised William he should first focus on improving his overall performance before applying for an internal position, but he decided to proceed with the posting anyway. Based on his subpar performance in his current role, he was not even selected for an interview.

The moral of this story is to be sure your performance is up to par because you never know when an opportunity will be available to you. I'm sure William was qualified technically for the job, but his lackadaisical attitude in his current position led to poor performance and a missed opportunity at a new job. His attitude also contributed to his poor attendance record, which was another red flag with the tentative department. Fast forward one year later—William learned from this experience and began to consistently meet performance expectations. He kept his performance and attendance at an acceptable level so that he would be ready at the drop of a hat. When another posting opportunity became available in that same department, William posted for the job, interviewed, and was offered the position!

Call center flashback: I acquired a new team and soon after met with team member Fitz to discuss his monthly performance. Rather quickly during our conversation, Fitz informed me he was ready to get off the phones and move to another role. I congratulated him on his career aspirations and proceeded to ask some probing questions. Even though I knew the answers, I wanted to see where Fitz's mind-set was. I asked Fitz how his attendance and performance were in his current role. He proceeded to say his results should be fine, but when I shared his results and compared them to the goals, it was evident Fitz's overall performance and attendance were not in line with established goals. I shared with Fitz that it is great to aspire to better opportunities, but he must first be sure to have solid performance in his current role. Fitz was challenged to improve his overall performance by taking more time to ensure great quality and to eliminate distractors that were negatively impacting his quality. Unfortunately, Fitz did not take heed of the coaching provided and continued with subpar performance and poor attendance. Eventually, opportunities for different roles became available, but Fitz's performance would not warrant him consideration for the new role. Because Fitz was not ready, he missed an opportunity to change roles.

Are you a team player? As mentioned earlier in this book, call centers are usually segmented by teams in which individual results as well as overall team performance are tracked. The team's overall quality, productivity, and compliance should be at a certain level in order to meet expectations. So this means each person should pull his or her weight in order for the team to meet or exceed goals. I have seen team members miss all performance metrics and not even bat an eye when they continually miss individual results. In my mind I am saying, "Really?" I expected them to acknowledge their lacking performance, but they didn't seem to care about the impact their results had on the team and, most important, how their results spoke to them as individuals. On the other hand, when a team member does not meet goals but is putting forth a true effort to do so, team members are more willing to encourage and help that team member improve. This is teamwork at its best!

People skills are vital in the workplace. Experts confirm a large percentage of job success comes from interpersonal skills. Have you seen someone with excellent product knowledge and technical skills but poor people skills? Because of poor people skills, they can't be trusted to represent the company's brand and are typically passed over for promotional opportunities. If you find yourself in this predicament, it can take a long time for your employer to feel confident with your interpersonal skills. You will need to genuinely inspect your workplace actions and how others perceive you. Again, it might take a while before management notices your change in attitude is genuine, so don't give up. Keep pressing! Now if you have demonstrated a sustained change and management still does not recognize it, you might need to consider new employment.

Call center flashback: It is always a privilege to have employees with a positive attitude on the team. They tend to see the big picture and will put forth an effort to adhere to company policies and procedures. The key words are attitude and effort; even if they struggle with meeting performance goals, their honest effort and attitude seem to be the redeeming factors. It's like that positive attitude compels you to be their number one cheerleader. You want to see them succeed. On the other hand, employees with a negative attitude can be mentally draining and consume most of your time. They have concerns about most processes instead of taking a collaborative approach by providing recommendations with a positive and open-minded attitude. Ellen was an employee with a positive attitude, and she put forth a valiant effort to meet her performance metrics daily. The only metric she struggled with was productivity. We discussed ways to improve her productivity; she job shadowed with others, and subject matter experts provided her with feedback on the way she served her customers. Even though she continued to struggle, I noticed an admirable trait with Ellen: perseverance. On a daily basis, Ellen would come to my desk to get her current Average Handle Time (AHT). On her way to lunch, she wanted an update on her performance, and then again she would ask for an update on her last break. At the end of her shift, Ellen would drop by to get a final update on her AHT for the day. It got to a point that any time Ellen came to my desk I would automatically pull her stats. I could tell she was trying her best and, guess what, she eventually made improvement with her AHT.

Dependability

Reporting to work when expected and on time is critical to the success of any business, especially call centers, because employees need to be available to handle the phone calls. Remember that most call centers have specific service objectives that should be met on a consistent basis. With this in mind, it is important for employees to return from their breaks and lunch on time in order to be available to answer incoming calls. Unfortunately, some employees will take a few minutes or even longer on their breaks, and others are slow to fully log back on the phones to resume taking calls. What does this mean? The representatives' adherence will be negatively impacted and the ability to meet service levels is minimized. You might think, *"But I was only five minutes late. What's the big deal?"* In a call center, you must have a big picture view because the dynamics of a call center are exponential. Individual issues have a bigger impact because of the large number of employees involved. If everyone in a call center of 150 employees is five minutes late, you are looking at twelve and a half hours of lost productivity. Think about how much work could be completed or how many customers could be served during this lost time. To be honest, this example is rather conservative. A considerable number of employees greatly exceed five minutes in their breaks, lunch breaks, and tardies to work. A more realistic example would be an average overage of twenty minutes with the same population of 150 employees; this equates to an astonishing fifty hours of lost productivity.

It's always best to have realistic expectations during your breaks. If you have a fifteen-minute break, it is unrealistic to make an important phone call that might run over your break time. Instead of making this important phone call during a short break, wait until your lunchtime so that you are not rushed and your chances of being late are less likely. If you have a pattern of being late to work, determine what causes you to be late. Does it take you a long time to get dressed? Get your clothes ready the night before. If it's traffic, leave earlier or take another route. Whatever the reason, you should be able to address the issue. If you have a genuine dilemma, speak to management to see if your schedule can be adjusted.

When employees call out for their entire shift, you can imagine the impact on service and productivity. Of course, there are valid reasons why an employee will need to call out for his or her shift. That's why employers have attendance policies in place. However, when employees do not manage their callouts effectively, they will probably find themselves in some type of corrective action process. Always be mindful of how poor attendance impacts customers and coworkers as they have to pick up your slack. In my years working in call centers, one of the top reasons for terminations in a call center has always been poor attendance. It baffles the mind how some employees continue to call out and accumulate unscheduled absences, and when it gets to the point where they are placed on corrective action, they claim it's an unfair policy. Truth be told, some callouts are the result of our poor choices or poor planning. If we look back at all of the unscheduled callouts, a vast majority were avoidable; we just did not want to go to work or something else took precedence. It's frustrating to see a seemingly able-bodied person abuse the company's attendance policy; some will use any reason to validate their absence or tardy. These individuals usually find themselves in some type of attendance policy violation. On the other hand, there is another population of employees who will strive to honor their work schedules even through sickness or tragedy because they have such a strong work ethic. It might be a therapeutic intervention to have those with a strong work ethic mentor someone with a slack work ethic, especially in the area of attendance. The person with the strong work ethic can share best practices on what they do to ensure good attendance.

You can typically pinpoint employees with attendance/dependability issues; just take a look at their paid time off (PTO) usage. Depending on the employer, employees will earn or accrue paid time off at set intervals. Some employers will grant a set amount of vacation time at the beginning of the calendar year, and at a specific point employees will accrue paid time off for the rest of the year. As long as the employees do not use their time, it will continue to accrue during the year. In order for employees to take a full week's vacation, they will need to use their accrued time, which is part of their compensation package. Some employees properly plan their accrued time and can comfortably take their planned vacations. Attendance policies usually specify that if employees cannot work their shifts, any accrued time will be used to cover the absence. Those employees with poor attendance cannot accrue a substantial amount of paid time off because it is consistently being absorbed by the unscheduled callouts they have. They will also encounter instances when their unscheduled callouts may be coded as unscheduled time off without pay because they have exhausted any accrued time, so they will not be paid for the unscheduled absence. I don't know about you, but I need a steady paycheck!

I once heard a minister say that people with chronic dependability issues should stop making excuses and make adjustments. Stop blaming the traffic, stop blaming the children, stop blaming the car, and take ownership by making the necessary adjustments. The takeaway is maintaining a good attendance record requires discipline and much needed planning in order to honor the commitment made when we accepted the job offer.

Call center flashback: I remember one day I woke up stressed and dreaded going to work. I got dressed and was on my way to work, but I just could not make that turn down the street to get to the job. I kept driving up and down the avenue and eventually had to call my friend/advocate at the job, who talked me through my "moment." I eventually made it to work—a bit late, but I made it! I did not have an attendance issue, so this tardy was not a concern to my manager. I probably could have called out for the day, but I pressed on. What's the moral of this story? Sometimes we don't feel like going to work. If you can afford to take that mental day off and you have properly managed your attendance record, more power to you! But if you have found yourself with excessive unscheduled absences, you need to press on and get to work.

At times, we have an unexpected situation; if it does not take the full day, handle the issue and go to work. Most attendance policies count absences based on the number of hours missed. Being absent a full day is weighted more than being late three hours, so remember this option when faced with unexpected situations.

I do believe employees with continual attendance issues had poor attendance during high school. Either their parents/guardians did not enforce the importance of going to school, or they played hooky often. I have seen employees call out one day and come to work the next day with a full-blown new hairdo! Of course my thought is they called out just to get their hair done. If you are going to disregard the company's attendance policies and call out when you please, then be prepared to accept the consequences of being placed on corrective action and possibly missing out on a pay raise or losing your job. Don't get mad at your supervisors—they have to ensure equity within their team.

Call center flashback: Keith was a very pleasant and well-liked person. He maintained a positive working relationship with his coworkers and management. When it came to his soft skills with his customers, Keith was top-notch! He presented a warm and engaging tone to his customers when he was at work. The operative phrase for Keith was, "When he was at work." Attendance and timeliness were his issues. Keith had a trend of reporting to work late as well as taking longer breaks and lunch. It was a daily issue—he could not get to work on time and consistently returned from break or lunch late. Unfortunately, he progressed through the corrective action process, but he still could not correct the behavior. Because Keith was such a likeable person, the employer tried to work with him by offering to slightly adjust his schedule. Unfortunately, Keith could not correct the behavior and the decision was made to terminate him because of poor attendance. What a sad situation for Keith. He had a family he had to support, and I'm sure the income from the job was a substantial contribution to help make ends meet. But that source of income was cut off abruptly because of his own inability to understand the importance of dependability.

Call center flashback: Samantha was always mindful of attendance. In fact, she had perfect attendance and had great compliance. Samantha submitted a request for time off, but unfortunately it was not approved because the maximum time-off slots were already filled. She had family plans and really needed the time off. I advised Samantha if she called out during this time she would still be considered in good standing because of her excellent attendance record. She decided that she would not come to work and take the occurrence. As with most companies, if you are not going to report to work, you must officially notify your supervisor, so I reminded her to be sure to call if she would not be at work. On the day Samantha was going to miss work, she called and left me a voicemail. I must tell you, her message made me chuckle because I could tell she felt uneasy about missing work. When Samantha returned to work, she admitted the entire process of calling out stressed her. She said she would never do that again! But I reminded her that because she properly managed her attendance she was able to call out and still have an excellent attendance record. Samantha, thank you for demonstrating dependability on a consistent basis! You truly understand how your presence helps keep call volume manageable.

FMLA Abuse

The Family Medical Leave Act (FMLA) entitles eligible employees of covered employers to take job-protected leave and unpaid time for specified family and medical reasons. FMLA provides coverage for specified time frames for the following reasons: personal or family illness, family military leave, pregnancy, adoption, or the foster care placement of a child.

This act was passed in 1993 during the Clinton administration with the intent to help balance the demands of the workplace with the needs of families. I personally believe this is an excellent benefit to those employees who qualify for such coverage. On a sad note, I have seen instances in which employees have abused FMLA, which is also an integrity issue as discussed earlier. When FMLA was in its early stages, there was rampant abuse because employers might not have required regular documentation to support an FMLA absence. I recall instances in which employees with FMLA coverage appeared to abuse this benefit because they did not want to come to work and word would get back to the job that they were seen out and about during the day. I use the word "appear" because I don't want to come across as judgmental or lacking positive intent. But it is safe to say some employees have abused FMLA, which resulted in corrective action or even termination. Employers are now becoming more aware of FMLA abuse and are implementing better processes and documentation requirements to support the absence. On a positive note, I have had discussions with employees who do not abuse their FMLA coverage, which shows strong integrity on their part. They understand this allowance was granted as a benefit for their particular situation, so they will not abuse it. Thank you to those who conscientiously utilize their FMLA or disability benefits!

Another company benefit employees can abuse is the use of short-term disability. This is a form of employee or group insurance coverage that pays a percentage of an employee's salary during the time the employee cannot work. Unfortunately, some employees will use short-term disability for reasons other than medically necessary and more for selfish reasons. Granted, I would say the majority of short-term disability claims are valid and a worthwhile benefit for employees. On the other hand, some employees will abuse short-term disability and follow the usually extended appeals process in order to extend their absence or use this time to find another job, thereby never returning to the job.

Call center flashback: As part of a team-building initiative, the supervisor team went out for lunch and a minor league baseball game. Rewind several hours earlier. Connor, a customer service representative, was protected under FMLA and called out to take care of a covered event. The supervisor team had a nice lunch and made it to the baseball park a bit early in order to get tickets and snacks. While waiting for the game to begin, the supervisor team was talking and joking with each other when whispers in disbelief filtered within the group. Whispers of "Is that Connor at the game?"; "I thought he called out under FMLA."; "Why would he show up at the game?"; "OMG, he's coming our way!"

As fate would have it, Connor proceeded to move to his seat, which was located next to the supervisor team. Awkward! Connor was flabbergasted; some supervisors were confused; and others were straight out amused. Connor's supervisor approached him to inquire why he was at the game when he called out under FMLA. Connor said he took care of the issue and decided to take in the game. Actually Connor should have taken care of his business and made his way to work as this would have shown positive intent on his part. Unfortunately, his actions gave an impression that he was abusing the FMLA coverage granted to him.

Call center flashback: Call centers also have employees who take pride in their performance. They put forth a grand effort to meet or exceed expectations. They report to work when expected and return from breaks and lunch on time. Jennie was a new hire and immediately displayed all the IPAD qualities. She could be counted on to follow established policies, she was ethical in her actions, and she presented professional behavior, a positive attitude, and excellent attendance. She was the total package! Jennie's focus on her job and workplace maturity excluded her from the drama that can be prevalent in the workplace. Jennie knew how to effectively navigate her actions and performance; as a result, she earned a performance bonus the first time she became eligible! I would jokingly tell Jennie I wished that I could clone her. As mentioned previously, there are a lot of "Jennies" in call centers. To all the Jennies out there, thank you! Your continued contributions are always appreciated.

Call center flashback: This flashback is an all-inclusive. Gracie was on my team a short time when I realized she was the poster child for a high-maintenance employee. High-maintenance employees require and seek out more attention than other employees. Their needs are immediate and they typically have numerous issues or concerns regarding work policies. High-maintenance employees have a difficult time picking their battles, which comes across as if they are not happy with anything and should be the center of attention. Basically, high-maintenance employees are draining to the supervisor. If Gracie needed a day off, it was urgent and she could not wait for the request to be reviewed. Even as a new employee, Gracie was bold enough to approach senior management to approve her time off instead of going through the proper protocol. I recall the time I scheduled my initial meeting with Gracie just to welcome her to the team and discuss our expectations of each other. I was flabbergasted when Gracie appeared nibbling on a cup of sunflower seeds still in the shell! I shared with Gracie that I would not show up to a meeting nibbling on sunflower seeds. She did discard them and apologized for her behavior. Gracie was too familiar with her coworkers; she shared too much of her personal life with too many people, which is not a good idea in the workplace. Eventually, there was an argument with one of her so-called friends and harsh words were exchanged. Gracie seemed to be the common denominator with issues; she had to be monitored closely to ensure she was taking calls when expected and she had a bad habit of eating meals at her desk, which was against company policy. Basically, she was a busybody at work for all the wrong reasons. She soon established a reputation of being immature and a difficult person to manage.

Chapter 7

What's Your Customer Service Portrait?

With face-to-face customer service, customers have the added advantage of visualization to determine their overall customer experience. They can factor in facial expressions and body language in addition to verbal interactions and accuracy. When dealing with a customer service representative over the phone, customers do not have the visual aspect, so they will heavily rely on the representative's tone of voice, willingness to help, and the ability to accurately resolve the issue in a timely manner. With these behaviors, callers will create a customer service portrait of how they believe the representative behaves or looks. Let's paint some portraits using the following examples. The portrait results are the customers' view of the representative based on how they were serviced.

Portrait 1

Representative behaviors:

- The representative speaks to the customer in a flat, monotone voice.
- The representative does not fully answer the customer's question.
- The customer makes brief comments about the great weather—the representative does not respond or acknowledge.

Portrait results (how customers picture the representative based on how they were served):

A customer service representative without a smile and with a mean look on his or her face, not personable, and not interested in their job. The representative is slouched in his or her seat, not attentive.

Portrait 2

Representative behaviors:

- The representative speaks with positive words.
- The representative changes his or her pitch through the use of voice inflection.
- The customer is frustrated about a policy—the representative sincerely apologizes and takes time to ensure the customer understands the policy by explaining further.
- The customer makes brief comments about a recent snowstorm—the representative acknowledges the comments.

Portrait results:

A customer service representative with a smile who is interested in helping his or her customer. The representative is sitting straight in his or her chair and working quickly to help the customer. He or she is friendly and caring. The customer will probably give a compliment on such great service.

Portrait 3

Representative behaviors:

- The representative provides conflicting information.
- The representative is slow with providing information and places the customer on hold for extended periods of time.
- When the customer asks additional questions, the representative does not provide much detail.

Portrait results:

A customer service representative who is frustrated and unorganized. One who does not have much product knowledge and is not trustworthy. The customer will probably call back or ask to speak to a supervisor.

Portrait 4

Representative behaviors:

- The representative sighs when the customer asks additional questions.
- The representative speaks in a condescending tone and speaks very fast.
- The representative uses negative words during the call. ("We don't do that here," "I can't help you with that.")

Portrait results:

A representative with an arrogant and sarcastic personality. A mean-spirited person who does not like his

or her job. The customer will probably end the call and
call back again or it will lead to a complaint.

This would also be a great team exercise to reveal how the
representatives' actions affect the way customers view them.
Have prerecorded calls that include great and poor customer
service or have team members play the role of a customer and
customer service representative where they act out typical
calls. Using a flip chart (or multiple flip charts depending on
the size of the team), the other team members will sketch a
customer service portrait of the representative based on how
he or she served the customer.

Unfortunately, customers can make biased assumptions
that can distort their portrait of the representative. Such
negative biases can be based on the representative's name or
dialect. It's not fair, but it happens. I had a representative on my
team with a distinct dialect, but you could clearly understand
what this person was saying. Sadly, some of the customers did
not want to be served by this person and requested to speak
to someone else because of preconceived notions. If you find
yourself in this situation, strive to show the customer your
capabilities early in the conversation. This can be done through
the use of positive/can-do phrases or actions that can break
down their defenses.

Chapter 8

Supervisor Amnesty Day

Earlier in this book, we discussed that most call centers are comprised of teams overseen by supervisors. A team consists of various personality and performance types, which can make the responsibility of managing a team rather complex. The supervisor wants to make sure everyone feels they are being treated the same, but on the same note, the supervisor must appeal to each team member's individuality. Some team members are pretty much self-managed and require minimum corrective coaching. However, some require consistent monitoring, follow-up, or informal and formal coaching on behavior or performance issues.

To the supervisor, this can be a frustrating position. It makes the supervisor question employees' motives; are they really trying to improve or do they not care about their job? The supervisor might begin to feel he or she is investing more than the employees are giving because of minimal improvement in performance, behavior, or attitudes. When a pattern of low performance or poor behavior is evident, employees will need to go through a formal coaching process. The formal coaching process entails some type of dialogue with employees to outline expectations followed with the necessary up-training. The formalized coaching process can progress through the various steps, which can ultimately end with termination of employment.

Some employees put forth a valiant effort and positive attitude throughout the coaching process, and then there are others. The "others" are resistant to improve, immature, or do not take ownership for their actions. It's important that discussions as well as documentations be politically correct and free of any biases or personal feelings management might have about the person or situation. It is common that human resources approves any formal corrective action documents in order to prevent employee complaints, grievances, or lawsuits. The documentations must have specific factual data, no opinions.

Supervisors who do not have the gift of a filter often find themselves involved in some type of grievance with employees. This is referred to as "foot in mouth" syndrome. Even during informal conversations with employees, management must be sure to speak in politically correct terms. At times, employees can say unfair or even hurtful comments to supervisors, but we must remain responsible with our responses—we are held to a higher standard.

Most supervisors have found themselves in a coaching situation where they wanted to vent their frustrations and say something very blunt to the employees. Wouldn't it be great if members of the management team could have an amnesty day when they could tell employees exactly what's on their minds without fear of any repercussions from human resources? I enlisted some of my fellow managers to share what they wish they could tell their employees— free from the human resources vernacular. Astonishingly, common themes emerged from my fellow peers who have worked at various call centers. Take a look at their wishful Freudian slips:

- You just don't want to come to work. Stop making excuses and come to work!

- You can't fit a right foot in a left shoe. Let's face it. You are just not cut out for this job!

- If you don't stop hanging up on your customers, I will take you out of this building by the scruff of your neck—with a quickness!

- You were hired to do a job; you were not hired to have a social hour at work.

- A nasty attitude at home is a nasty attitude at work.

- Why are you taking up space? Other people need a job and will try their best to meet goals.

- You should be ashamed of yourself! Stop abusing the company's FMLA and leave of absence benefit.

- So you want to be considered for other job opportunities? You are not even trying to meet goals in your current role!

- Stop being so difficult.

- Do you have any home training? Why are you behaving like this at work?

- Why do you wear tight clothes? This is not a nightclub!

- Stop talking about your personal business at work. Your so-called friends are talking about you behind your back!

- Another bereavement? How many grandmothers do you have?

- So if the doctor has you on bed rest, why are you in the office asking for your check? If this was my company, you would be terminated right now!

- I cannot believe you just said that to that caller. Does the word "recorded" mean anything to you?

- *Ahhh*! My life is complete. You actually decided to show up to work today!

- I have tried to get you to change off the record but because you won't do better, now I have to beat you with a pen (formal documentation/corrective action)!

- A supervisor asked why an employee couldn't get to work on time. The employee said it was because of the devil. "Well, you better get this straightened out with the devil, or you will lose your job!"

- Why must I remind you to perform your basic responsibilities? The world does not revolve around you!

- An employee tells a supervisor she believes she does not like her. Supervisor: "I am not your mother; I'm not here to like you."

- A supervisor has an out-of-body experience when coaching employees on behavior issues. "You can say or do anything on your last day. Is this your last day?"

- An employee is constantly complaining about the company and not taking any ownership of his performance. The supervisor would normally try to encourage the employee to keep a positive attitude. I wish I could say, "Why don't you do me a favor and quit!"

- Yes, there is a mute button. No, you did not press it. Yes, the customer called back to complain. No, you do not have a job!

- Are you Cray-Cray?

- An employee is being coached on historically poor attendance. The supervisor is aware the employee had attendance problems with a previous job and asks the employee about attendance problems in the past. The employee says he did not have any attendance issues before. Supervisor: "Stop lying, Pinocchio! Your previous supervisor told me you had poor attendance!"

- You will be late to your own funeral!

- An employee is known for requesting to adjust the work schedule each week. Supervisor: "Do you know the meaning of a schedule? It means you work the hours you were given!"

- Bye, Felisha!

- Here comes drama!

- Do you know your jeans are too tight? What were you thinking when you walked out of your house?

- The truth will eventually come to light—you know what you are doing!

- How many foot surgeries can you get? . . . You only have two feet!

- I'm gonna leave my badge on the desk and you are gonna leave your badge on the desk. We gonna step outside but only one of us is coming back in. If *you* come back in, you just got *promoted*. If *I* come back in, I just got *demoted*.

- Why is all your FMLA time around holidays, school planning days, and on Fridays and Mondays? How convenient!

- Employee: "I can't talk on the phone today . . . my throat hurts . . . I don't feel good. Do you have something off the phone I can do?" Supervisor: "Yes, as a matter of fact, you can go home!"

- Grow up, or quit, because you are bringing the entire team down, and I'm just tired of dealing with such an immature person!

- No one owes you anything. You have to earn it!

- You are in the workplace. Pull up your pants!

Chapter 9

How to Improve Your Customer Service Skills

I hope that by now you have considered your ways and con- cluded there might be some room for improvement with your customer service skills, work ethic, or professionalism in the workplace. So what are the next steps? Well, the first step is a critical one: admitting there is an issue that needs to be addressed. Congratulations! Just as with an addiction multi- step program, the first step is to admit you have a problem. Now, I'm not comparing this to an addiction recovery process, but accepting the fact there is an opportunity for improvement is a major step in any healing process. The next phase is to take some proactive measures to correct these areas. When we were in grade school, we were taught to remember our vowels. Let's use these vowels to help us remember the core standards of customer service and how we can achieve exceptional perfor- mance in the workplace.

A	ADVOCATE
E	EDUCATE
I	INITIATIVE
O	OWNERSHIP
U	UNDERSTAND

Advocate

Everyone needs someone who will encourage you, celebrate with you, and provide honest and candid feedback when your performance or attitude is lacking. Your advocate will fulfill this very crucial role. *Merriam-Webster* defines an advocate as one who supports or promotes the interests of another. If you do something well, your advocate will acknowledge that. On the other hand, your advocate should call you out when you are going down the wrong path. So it is critical to find that person who will be able to acknowledge the high points as well as share the opportunities for improvement. Your advocate should feel empowered and comfortable enough in providing such candid feedback. They should be a person who demonstrates professionalism with a strong work ethic. Bottom line: you want an advocate to practice what he or she preaches. Your role is to remain open-minded and receptive to your advocate's feedback. Put all defenses aside and focus on the end product—a better you! If you are fortunate enough to sit next to someone who demonstrates excellent customer service skills with a professional outlook, ask them to mentor you.

If you ever worked in a call center, you might have witnessed situations where a representative was rude, loud, or not helpful to their customers. The coworkers sitting by would laugh and chuckle while the representative put on a show of unprofessional antics. I envision a true advocate would try to calm down their coworkers and help them retain composure so that the call is not further escalated. Why would you let your coworker continue on a downward spiral with a call that is possibly recorded and could lead to a complaint, corrective action, or even termination? What we tend to do when we are not happy in our job is to find someone in our same state. We want someone to agree with our plight and justify our negative behaviors. Rather, we should find that valuable advocate who will challenge us to see the big picture. We all need to be accountable to someone; make sure that someone is a role model. A person who will push you to excellence. A person who will prick your conscience to do better and inspire you for greatness! We truly are our brother's keeper.

Educate

Education is a lifelong experience; there is always something to learn, especially on the job. Take time to learn your company's customer service guidelines and procedures. Become the company's subject matter expert in a particular field as this will make you a more valuable employee. During low call volume, review policies and procedures between calls. This would be a better option than holding side conversations with coworkers. Don't be so quick to take VTO but rather use this time to build your knowledge base (voluntary time off is offered during very low call volume). I would encourage my team to "luxuriate" during low call volume and use this time to learn something new. Unfortunately, I've seen representatives lay their heads on their desks, read personal books, crochet, or even work on extreme couponing projects. Use your time wisely and reinvest in yourself! Explore the company's online resources for information and self-study courses that can supplement your knowledge. Talk to your supervisors as they might have knowledge of other company resources available for your development. On a more global format, ponder enrolling in courses through your local college or university. Most companies offer a tuition reimbursement program in which employees are repaid handsomely for successfully completing covered courses. Tuition reimbursement is a wonderful company benefit that can be used to obtain a higher learning degree. Even if you are not looking to obtain a degree, your employer might be willing to sponsor some business-related courses for your personal development.

Initiative

Take the initiative to set up your reference material in a way in which you can learn it. Don't depend on your supervisor or trainer to be your everything. Everybody learns differently and the standard training process might not fit your style, so craft your learning in a way that will help you retain information more efficiently. Be sure to take the initiative and let your supervisors know if you need additional training on a specific subject. They can either provide you the necessary up-training or have a subject matter expert provide the training. Don't sit back and wait for someone to read your mind; take the initiative to do your due diligence or reach out to someone who can help you. And always remember you might need to do a follow-up on a request if you did not get a response the first time or so. Don't think the person is avoiding you; he or she might have just honestly forgotten or not had the time to address your request. Take the initiative to make recommendations on process improvements. As a customer service representative, you are the front line to the customer and can provide call trends or system glitches to management. At times, you might be frustrated because work processes might not be effective or efficient. Talk to your manager about your ideas and suggestions. On a side note: Managers, listen to your employees. They might have a practical solution to an ongoing problem. Even if the idea is not feasible, be sure to have some type of dialogue with them.

Ownership

We should take accountability for our actions and realize how such actions impact others. We all have an idea of our areas of opportunities. Take ownership of these opportunities and take the appropriate action to correct them. If you have an attendance issue, own the issue and take the necessary steps to correct the behavior. This might be as simple as leaving fifteen minutes earlier to ensure you make it to work on time. If your tone comes across as curt or rude, make a concentrated effort to change that behavior. During my years coaching associates on maintaining a positive tone, I have heard responses such as, "Well, Ms. Gwen, this is how I sound," or, "I can't change how I speak." Instead of making excuses, practice softening your delivery through the use of positive phrases and voice inflection. Voice inflection is done by changing the pitch in your speech as opposed to sounding flat and monotone. If you tend to get more complaints and escalations than others, take ownership that you might be doing something that ignites emotions to make the customer want to speak with someone else. Don't be fooled by thinking all of the difficult and angry customers are being routed to you. No, the real issue might be that you are not utilizing the soft skills needed to effectively resolve customer inquiries.

Own your performance. Picture your current job as a "training ground" or "preparation" for your next move. Even though this might not be your dream job, you should still work as if it was. Treat your job as if you owned the company. I'm sure if you were the owner of the company, you would not allow such negative behaviors in your workplace. You would see how every employee's performance contributes to overall company results.

Understand

Understand the goal is to be a better you! It's also for you to pass the torch and be a positive example to others in the workplace. Understand that others are watching you and how you do your job. In a time when the job market is extremely competitive, there might come an opportunity when a business associate might be in a position to refer you for a job. Do you think a business associate would recommend you for a job if you demonstrated a poor work ethic with a previous employer? You are missing out on possible referrals, promotions, and other business connections because you did not present yourself in a positive light.

Understand, you are a walking resume. Your attitudes, interpersonal skills, and job performance are all on show. Your actions in the breakroom are noticed just as keenly as your actions in the boardroom. It's amazing that, when we interview for a job, we take all opportunities to convince the recruiter we are the best fit for the company. We speak to our ability to properly serve customers and we provide convincing evidence that we are dependable and understand the importance of reporting to work when expected and on time. But, when we get the job, we get too comfortable and forget about the full court press we presented during the interview. We do not take the extra effort to meet performance goals; we work with a lack of motivation and we complain about the company without making valuable contributions or recommendations for improvements. Understand that your supervisor should not have to force, plead, or beg for you to do your job. You should have the basic instinct to want to maintain good performance in the workplace.

Call center flashback: Many moons ago, human resources had the sole responsibility for hiring staff, but that role has become a mutual partnership. Human resources or an outsourced company might process applications and conduct phone interviews while leaving the actual face-to-face interviews for the actual business unit. This is a smart move because who else would know the type of employees needed to fill the role? I've always felt I was a good judge of character when performing interviews, but there are always instances when the educated decision to hire someone is misguided by the crafty interviewee who knows how to effectively navigate through an interview. Case in point. Carl applied for a customer service representative job and was granted an onsite interview. I went to greet Carl in the lobby and the first impression was great! He was well dressed and personable. Carl's resume did not have any gaps of employment; he provided appropriate responses to the interview and had previous customer service experience. Based on what he presented, he appeared to be a good fit for the role, and, as a result, Carl was offered the job. After Carl transitioned from training to the live floor environment, I began to notice some performance issues such as taking extended breaks and lunch as well as not being at his desk when expected. He would have multiple system issues but was not actively trying to correct the issues to resume taking calls. I've always tried to keep tabs on those I recommended to hire in order to track my success rate as an interviewer. I talked to Carl's supervisor to get an update on his performance and was saddened to find out his performance was subpar across the board. Did I miss any glaring opportunities during the interview, or was Carl well versed on proper interview protocol? I don't know the answer to this million-dollar question, but the struggle continues with finding the right person for the job!

Chapter 10
Employer Obligations

I t is a fact that a business has obligations to its customer base; without customers, a business can't thrive. Another important obligation of a business is to its employees. As mentioned earlier in this book, employers typically have established core values or mission statements that dictate how they should conduct business with the public and their employees. The employer–employee relationship is an agreement of sorts; the employer compensates employees for the work or services they perform. The first obligation of an employer is to make sure the business hires the right people for the job. There are times when an employer is faced with an aggressive hiring plan which means employees need to be hired and trained rather quickly. This could result in less than effective interviews where unqualified candidates are hired. It is vital that an employer does not submit to the "warm body" model where the company hires anyone just to fill a seat. Instead, the employer should plan sufficient time for the recruiters and hiring managers to hire the right people. The employer should also invest in proper training for those who will perform the interviews.

Have you interviewed for a job where the employer provided a list of reasons why you should work for the company? The employer shares all of the positive aspects of the company as well as career opportunities and community initiatives. Some companies pretty much live up to the hype—they provide solid training and remain in touch with the new hire during the on-boarding process. Other companies have opportunities in this area; the training/on-boarding process is too swift or not conducive to various learning styles. We all know of some companies that have eliminated or condensed their training programs in efforts to increase their financial bottom lines. Or, because they need the new hires on the phone to help with call volume, they will forgo valuable training.

The employer should provide their employees with certain inalienable rights: training, competitive compensation, appreciation, and safe work conditions. At times, the employer does not get it right. The employer fails employees, which contributes to ill-equipped employees who are not able to meet performance expectations and uphold the core values/mission statements that the employer outlined. Once employees get frustrated and become disengaged, absenteeism increases and quality decreases. The employees have "checked out," and it will be a challenge for them to provide the excellent service customers expect. It is at this point when a company culture can take a turn for the worse; the frustrations can grow and fester, resulting in disengaged employees.

Employers need to listen to their employee base and invest in their employees' overall well-being with benefits and services that keep them whole—at work as well as away from work. Most employers now offer employee assistance programs where their employees can reach out for counseling and work-life balance guidance. Employees should take advantage of these programs in efforts to help create a successful work and life environment. Employers are also using yearly engagement surveys to get a temperature check on their employee base. Other ways an employer can remain in touch include holding periodic town hall meetings or skip-level meetings where the employees have the opportunity to get company updates and ask questions of senior management. Word of caution, employers: there should not be any lip service here—honor your word and obligations to your employees.

The main purpose at any call center is to handle phone calls, whether inbound or outbound. When there is heavy call volume in a call center, customer service representatives have very minimal time for up-training. The truth of the matter is that call volume takes precedence. It is common to see team meetings and training cancelled because of high call volume. It's the nature of the beast in a call center and will continue to be a challenge in balancing call volume with up-training opportunities for employees. Employers have established training curriculums that outline courses employees should take as well as recommended time frames. This is a great way to ensure employees receive consistent training and are prepared to serve their customers.

However, an employer should remember all employees are not the same and might not require the cookie-cutter training approach. Some employees need additional training, and it is up to the supervisor to identify and recommend those courses that will enhance employees' performance. As discussed, people come from different backgrounds and experiences, and it's easy to think people should have basic abilities in adulthood, but that might not be the case. Remember, some people can't do better because they don't know better. This is why the role of a supervisor is so critical. You should strive to build positive relationships with each member on your team; it is during these periods of engagement when you might be able to identify root causes of employee behaviors. I tell you, it's rewarding when employees can take that ownership and begin their journey to greatness!

Employers need to be mindful of the way employees are managed. Management styles range from very rigid to too lenient. My personal opinion is the best style lies somewhere in the middle. If a supervisor is too rigid, he or she will miss out on building positive relationships with their team members. The team members will most likely not want to do anything extra for such a supervisor; they will probably do just enough to keep the supervisor off their backs. On the other hand, if a supervisor is too lenient, some employees will not make significant contributions to the team. Team members might feel there is no need to strive for excellence, so they might begin to demonstrate slack in their work. I have worked with some supervisors who seem to enjoy terminating employees or placing them on corrective action. It's like they have a "gotcha" mentality when employees' behavior or performance need to be formally addressed. I have also seen supervisors who allowed their team to run amok, which oftentimes leads to unproductive results.

When you think of excellent customer service, which companies do you think of? Several companies are known for their dedicated focus to customer service; the two I think of are The Ritz-Carlton and Chick-fil-A. Both not only communicate excellent expectations but also live and breathe these principles in a consistent manner. In 2000, The Ritz-Carlton opened a public university for other organizations to learn the business practices that made The Ritz-Carlton a sustained leader in customer service excellence. The Ritz-Carlton Leadership Center prides itself on helping a significant number of organizations change their culture and improve customer service. Chick-fil-A is known for its prompt and friendly service. It seems like its employees genuinely enjoy their work. How do they find the right people? I read Chick-fil-A goes through a rigorous interviewing process to make sure the employees are a true reflection of the company's values and expectations. Coincidently, it's documented that Chick-fil-A sent some of its owners, operators, and managers to The Ritz-Carlton Leadership Center for exposure to The Ritz-Carlton's business strategies on customer service and employee engagement (See http://ritzcarltonleadershipcenter. com/2014/02/chick-fil-a-making-fast-service-memorable).

Chapter 11

The Customer: The Good, the Bad, the Ugly

What is the main component of customer service? What can cause a business to thrive or to falter? Who can use word of mouth to celebrate or degrade a business? It's the customer. Without a substantial customer base, most of us will be without a job. The customer has evolved to have higher expectations with a WIIFM attitude: "What's In It For Me?" Gone are the days when businesses have customers for life. Customers want to see benefits such as rebates, discounts, and other loyalty perks in addition to excellent customer service. If they don't get the perks and excellent service, they can easily take their business to a competitor. There was also a time when companies took the position that the customer is always right. We now see customers who use unethical actions to get what they want. This type of customer base has contributed to the frustrations with working in the customer service industry. I recall a customer service issue that made national news. The customer had a high-end credit card and made excessive charges but would turn around and make excessive returns. It became such an ordeal to service the customer that the company decided to close her credit card privileges. Customers need to remember respect and integrity go *both* ways. God don't like ugly!

Earlier in this book we discussed how the burdens of life can impede a customer service representative's ability to effectively perform his or her job. The same can apply to customers. Customers too have burdens that can provoke them to act irrationally, such as sickness in the body, grief, or financial woes. So customer service representatives should not retaliate because they don't know what customers are going through. Bottom line, I do believe most customers are fair while others can be unrealistic and unethical. As a customer service professional, you will be required to navigate and tread water appropriately. Don't allow customers to make you lose your composure. Remember, some customers are counting on you to lose your cool and will use that as a ploy to get some type of discount on merchandise or services. But, I must say, I get it. As a customer I too have received poor customer service to the point I needed to vent my frustrations to the representative. However, there should be a limit on venting; there is no need for excessive rants and vulgar language.

In chapter 7, we discussed how customers paint portraits based on how the representative serves them. The representative's tone, willingness to help, and ability to resolve issues accurately and timely contribute to the portrait. Unfortunately, some customers will use "non-performance" cues to paint a negative portrait of the representative. They will use stereotypes such as the representative's name, accent, or dialect to determine if the representative has the ability or qualification to serve them. I have witnessed numerous occasions when customers used these unfair cues to assume who the person on the other side of the phone was and even to go as far as refusing to have that person service them. Every representative deserves a chance to prove his or her worth and ability in serving customers; he or she should not be judged with stereotypical mind-sets. The role of a customer service representative is an honorable job. The representative can learn the various backend departments and become a subject matter expert in his or her department. He or she can also use this knowledge to progress within the company. Unfortunately, some customers view this job as a subservient role and will speak to the representative as if he or she is beneath them. We also discussed how customers will use social media to share their experiences with the public—the good, bad, and the ugly.

Call center flashback: Just like with cyberbullying, where people harass others behind the safety of their computers, some call center customers have a similar frame of mind. I have witnessed customers use their education or expertise to degrade customer service representatives. The customer intimidates the representative by using exorbitant talk with a condescending tone instead of using that gift of knowledge in a constructive manner. Case in point, an attorney called to discuss his account and began to use terminology that was more appropriate in the courtroom instead of a customer service inquiry. This attorney was condescending with his knowledge and attempted to trivialize the work of the customer service representative. I have also heard customers make racial comments to representatives based on their name or method of speech and use these stereotypes to perceive how well they would be served. The end result of phone calls like these typically produces high emotions and frustrations from both parties.

Call center flashback: Monte was a knowledgeable and efficient customer service representative with a stunning African dialect. He had a wonderful personality accompanied with a professional and helpful attitude. When customers allowed Monte to address their needs, this typically resulted in a satisfied customer. On the other hand, when Monte greeted his customers, some would immediately ask to be transferred to someone else. Other customers would specifically request to speak to an American. This became very frustrating to Monte because these rejections were based on unfair biases or preconceived expectations and not his ability to handle the call. How short-minded customers can be to decide that someone can't be of service to them just because he or she is different. These actions prevented Monte from executing his duties and fine-tuning his craft.

Where Do We Go from Here?

This book has revealed opportunities in the area of customer service. There is a population of employees who do not care about their jobs or the customers they serve and the employees they work with. Some don't even care about working as a team—it's a selfish mentality with a lack of workplace maturity. Is a specific generation causing the downfall in customer service? I have heard it's mainly the younger generation because it doesn't have a strong work ethic. That is not always the case. We have seasoned employees who are set in their ways of workplace immaturity and are setting poor examples for the impressionable younger generation.

Some employers do not focus on building positive relationships with their employees. Some are so fixated on making profits they forget employees are an integral part of making profits.

Customer service has a negative image these days, but I can proudly confirm the majority of those who work in customer service take pride in what they do. During my years of working in customer service, I had the privilege of working with some of the most talented and dedicated individuals. They understand and appreciate the value of their contributions. They endure the harshness of angry customers and empathize with their fragile customers. They work hard to build positive relationships and willingly share their technical knowledge and best practices with coworkers. The majority understand the importance of dependability and report to work when expected. It's the minority of the call center employees who cause the majority of customer service issues. It's this minority who consume most of their supervisors' time with handling complaints, corrective coaching, and updating poor attendance and performance documents. It's an exhaustive journey working with those employees who lack workplace maturity.

Parents and guardians, it is mandatory to have work ethic conversations with your young adults entering the workplace. Make sure they understand they need to honor their commitment by reporting to work when expected. Share your experiences and consequences as a result of your poor behaviors. Help them start off on the right foot—encourage them to get their clothes ready and pack their lunch the night before. If need be, make sure they wake up and leave for work on time. Make sure they dress and act appropriately for the workplace. Be your young adult's advocate at home and make sure you practice what you preach! Even though they might be considered grown in age, they still need your help and guidance. I have heard parents say once their children turn eighteen, they are on their own. They pretty much cut the parental strings and let the children learn from experience. Why would you want your children to encounter unnecessary issues at work when they could learn from your experience? I do get it; there is a point when your young adult children must be accountable for their actions—let's just be sure they know the basics. I believe my daughter has a strong work ethic because we had those "work ethic" conversations based on my experiences and frustrations at work. So I do think having such dialogue with your young adults is a good thing.

We can all agree everyone will depend on the services of a customer service representative. It's part of society's fabric; we must conduct business with companies in order to have and maintain life's essentials. Customer service representatives play a critical role in keeping society tied to its needs and wants. Without customer service, what would we do? So the million-dollar question is: who is responsible for the decline in customer service? As this book has revealed, all parties have contributed to the decline in customer service: the employer, the employee, and the customer. Therefore, all three parties must take their rightful ownership to correct this dilemma. The employer has to remain in tune with the needs of employees by giving them the tools needed to effectively perform their jobs. The employer should also establish a regular dialogue with its employee base to make sure the employees are engaged and feel appreciated. It is imperative for the employer to set aside targeted funds to ensure employees can partake in appreciation events, community initiatives, and nice compensation packages. Employers should be sure their recruitment efforts are top notch and that they are hiring the right people for the job. Employees need to take their jobs more seriously and remember they are a *walking resume*; everything you do is on show. Employees' personal brand should be something they are proud of. Employees should also understand they were hired to do a job and make concentrated efforts to meet established goals. Last, the customer base should understand respect goes both ways and should stop provoking representatives to lose their composure. Stop the dishonest attempts to get something for free. We all have to coexist in this customer service world.

Phew! I think I'm done. I feel very strongly about proper customer service—it's a passion, one might say. It's my sincere desire this book pricks your heart to take a deep look into your behavior and make the necessary changes that will make you a more valuable and respected employee. Yes, no one is perfect, *present party included*, but we all must strive to do better. It's a daily investment in yourself—and how valuable is that! Please don't be "that" employee who is known to cause drama in the workplace. Don't be "that" employee who is not pulling his or her weight at work. Don't be "that" employee with a negative attitude. Don't be "that" employee who is not approachable and not willing to work as part of a team. Don't be "that" employee with negative behaviors that stick in your supervisor's craw. Instead, be "that" employee who will put forth an effort to do his or her best. Be "that" employee who demonstrates dependability by reporting to work when expected. Be "that" employee whom others look up to and respect.

For our new call center employees, remain positive and do the right thing. Always remember your IPAD when at work. Don't get caught up with call center drama that can interrupt or cancel your career growth. Remember there are disgruntled employees who want to recruit you to join their disgruntled team. They will try to fill your head with negativity and conspiracies. Don't allow someone to brainwash you with negativity; you should be able to have your own opinion, but be sure to keep an open mind. It is true that misery loves company. Flee from these life-sucking employees as they will drain your positive attitude and you will find yourself in a negative and stagnant mind-set while others who remained focused on their job are moving to the next stage in their life. Don't let the naysayers have this control over you. Don't take the bait! When they come to you with negativity, keep it positive. They will soon get the message and change their conversations around you.

What is the future of customer service? Companies are diversifying customer service options through online, e-mail, and mobile applications, all of which will reduce call volume through the traditional phone call method. But there will always be a need for customer service. Once everybody, no matter what their role, takes ownership in doing the right thing, I am optimistic excellence in customer service can prevail!

About the Author

Gwendolyn Foster Oglesby has more than fifteen years of experience managing the call center teams of various Fortune 500 companies. It was during this time that she realized her passion for customer service and began to cultivate her platform for customer service awareness.

As a native of Jacksonville, Florida—a city known for its concentration of call centers—Gwen began to notice that the dynamics, behaviors, and drivers within various centers were strikingly similar. She also noticed that some of these patterns led to missed promotional opportunities, formal administrative write-ups, or even termination of employment—all of which can affect one's ability to establish a successful and respectful career. It is her sincere desire that this book can empower employees to present a positive work ethic and professional image in the workplace.

Gwen holds a bachelor's degree in business administration from the University of North Florida in Jacksonville, Florida.